Living *Water*

a creative resource for the Liturgy

Treasure Seekers

YEAR A

Susan Sayers

with Father Andrew Moore

Illustrated by Arthur Baker

Kevin Mayhew

First published in 1998 by
KEVIN MAYHEW LTD
Rattlesden
Bury St Edmunds
Suffolk IP30 0SZ

0 1 2 3 4 5 6 7 8 9

ISBN 1 84003 218 9
Catalogue No. 1500200

The other titles in the *Living Water* series are		
Complete Resource Book	ISBN 1 84003 217 0	Cat. No. 1500199
Prayer of the Faithful	ISBN 1 84003 221 9	Cat. No. 1500203
Pearl Divers	ISBN 1 84003 219 7	Cat. No. 1500201
Gold Panners	ISBN 1 84003 220 0	Cat. No. 1500202

Cover photographs:
Two small children – courtesy of SuperStock Ltd, London
Background – courtesy of Images Colour Library Ltd, London
Cover design by Jaquetta Sergeant
Edited by Katherine Laidler
Typesetting by Louise Selfe
Printed in Great Britain

FOREWORD

For this age group the world is opening out from the immediate family circle, and full of possibilities. The children are becoming aware of familiar faces Sunday by Sunday. It can be a daunting prospect, and the way young children are met and welcomed, talked and listened to, when they first encounter the children's liturgy in your church, will have a profound effect on their spiritual growth. It is through the good humour, care and friendliness of those they meet that they will begin to realise how God loves them.

In all your planning, keep aware of how it will seem from the children's point of view. Is the area attractive and inviting? Does the furniture fit? Is the atmosphere orderly and therefore unthreatening? Are people talking at a speed they can cope with, and giving them time to reply without pressure? Do people genuinely seem to like them and want them to be happy? Is considerate love and fairness expressed in actions as well as in the teaching? Is it a place where they can relax and feel at home? Is it fun?

These things are so important because the children will be learning far more from the way things are done and from the people they work with, than from the actual teaching content, valuable as this obviously is. It is a good idea to review your aims and objectives annually, setting out for yourselves, the parents, and any helpers, what you are doing and why, what works well and what needs to be tried differently. If this regular review is built into the system there is no danger of outdated methods carrying on past their sell-by date just because things have always been done like that. A termly or annual training day is also helpful in refreshing leaders and preventing cases of burn-out.

This book provides you with ideas and materials for activities for young children, all based on the weekly Lectionary readings. The activity sheets often include something to think and talk about together, and you can select and adapt the ideas to suit your particular group. Vary the media the children work with – crayons, finger paints, sponge painting, printing, paper and fabric collage, chalks and pastels are all fun to use. Pray for the children and their families, and read the Bible passages before you plan, so as to incorporate your own valuable insights, and use the suggested games either as they stand or as starting points to help you think of other ideas of your own.

A few general ideas about story-telling:

- Tell the story from the viewpoint of a character in the situation. To create the time-machine effect, avoid eye contact as you slowly put on the appropriate cloth or cloak, and then make eye contact as you greet the children in character.

- Have an object with you which leads into the story – a water jug, or a lunch box, for instance.

- Walk the whole group through the story, so that they are physically moving from one place to another; and use all kinds of places, such as broom cupboards, under the stairs, outside under the trees, and so on.

- Collect some carpet tiles – blue and green – so that at story time the children can sit round the edge of this and help you place on the cut-outs for the story.

If parents are going to be staying with their children, involve them in the activities, or think over the possibility of having an adult discussion group in the same room, using the study material and discussion questions in the *Living Water* Complete Resource Book. Parents are encouraged to pray with their children during the week, using the worksheet prayers.

All the material in the book is copyright-free for non-commercial use in churches and schools.

SUSAN SAYERS
with Father Andrew Moore

ACKNOWLEDGEMENT

The publishers wish to express their gratitude to Kingsway's Thankyou Music, PO Box 75, Eastbourne, East Sussex, BN23 6NW for permission to include the extract from *5000+ hungry folk* by Ian Smale © 1985 (Eighteenth Sunday of the Year).

CONTENTS

SPECIAL FEASTS

*This book is dedicated to my family and friends,
whose encouraging support has been wonderful,
and to all those whose good ideas are included here for others to share.*

RECOMMENDED BIBLES

It is often a good idea to look at a passage in several different versions before deciding which to use for a particular occasion.

As far as children are concerned, separate Bible stories, such as those published by Palm Tree Press and Lion, are a good introduction for the very young. Once children are reading, a very helpful version is the *International Children's Bible* (New Century version) published by Word Publishing. Here children have a translation based on experienced scholarship, using language structure suitable for young readers, with short sentences and appropriate vocabulary. There is a helpful dictionary, and clear maps and pictures are provided.

ADVENT

FIRST SUNDAY OF ADVENT

Thought for the day

We are to wake up and make sure we stay ready for the second coming.

Readings

Isaiah 2:1-5
Psalm 121:1-2, 4-5, 6-9
Romans 13:11-14
Matthew 24:37-44

Aim

To learn the importance of being alert to God all the time.

Starter

Play this version of 'musical bumps'. Tell the children that when you show the red sign they stand still. Whenever the music stops they sit down. This will mean that they have to keep watching, as well as listening, while they jump up and down.

Teaching

Praise everyone for watching and listening so well in the game. It was because they were watching and listening so well that they knew when to stop and when to sit down. Explain that Jesus told his friends to watch and listen carefully – he will be pleased to see how well the children at (your town) can do it already!

Explain that you are going to tell them a story. Every time they hear the word 'Jesus', they put their hand up.

Now tell them this story.

The world God had made was very beautiful. It had blue sea and green grass, and flowers of red and yellow and pink and purple. There were furry animals, and shining fish, birds which sang songs, and frogs which croaked. There were people. There were clouds. There was sunshine and rain and snow. God loved the world he had made. But he saw that people were spoiling the world; they were choosing to hate one another instead of loving one another. Sometimes they chose well and were happy. Sometimes they chose to be selfish and made themselves and each other very unhappy.

'The people I have made need saving and rescuing,' thought God. 'I will come to save and rescue them.'

He got his people ready. 'Watch and listen carefully!' he told them. 'Then when I come to save you, you will recognise who I am.'

Some of the people kept listening and watching. As they grew old they passed the message on to their children. And they passed it on to *their* children – 'Keep watching and listening. One day God will come to us to save and rescue us.'

At last, God kept his promise and came among his people in person to save and rescue them. The people had been expecting a rich and powerful king, but God came among his people as a tiny baby, who was born in a stable and put to bed in the animals' hay. This baby, whose name was Jesus, was God's Son, who had come into the world to save and rescue us.

Not everyone recognised him, because he wasn't what they were expecting. But the ones who were used to listening out for the loving words of God, and the ones who were used to watching out for the loving kindness of God – they knew exactly who Jesus was, and they were very pleased to meet him!

Praying

Dear God,
the world is full of your love. *(trace big circle)*
Help us to listen out for it. *(cup ears)*
Help us to watch out for it. *(shade eyes and look around)*
Thank you for all the goodness and love
that we can hear and see. Amen.

Activities

On the worksheet they can draw small and big things they enjoy seeing and hearing. These can all be cut out and stuck on to a group picture, or hole-punched and hung on to a coat hanger mobile, like this:

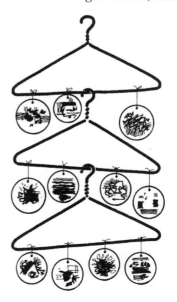

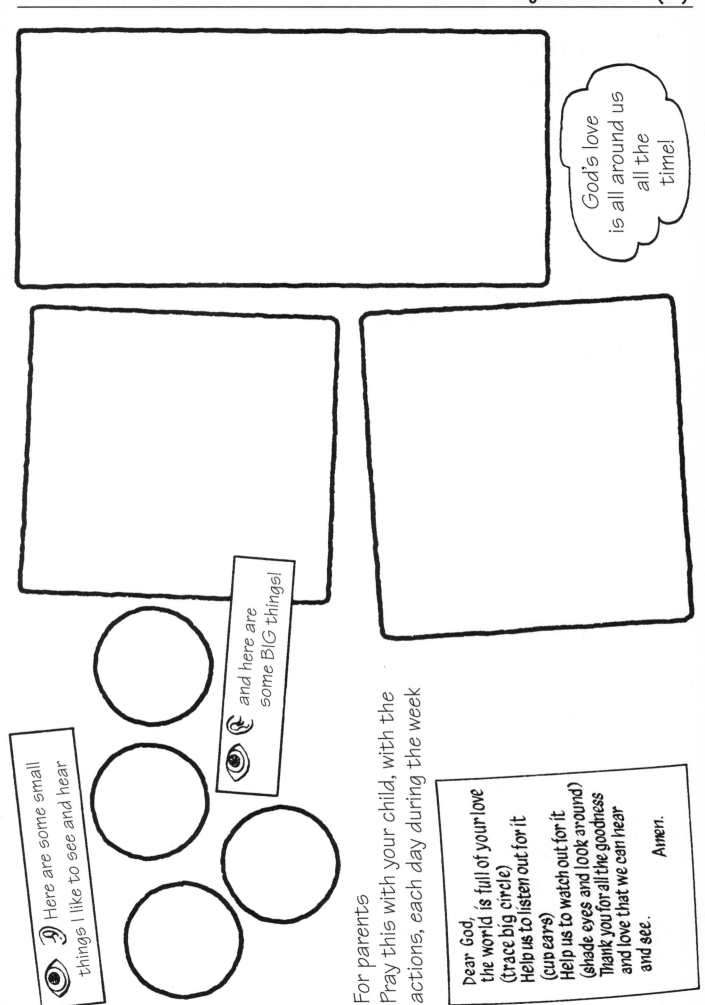

God's love
is all around us
all the
time!

👁🐭 Here are some small
things I like to see and hear

👂 and here are
some BIG things!

For parents
Pray this with your child, with the
actions, each day during the week

Dear God,
the world is full of your love
(trace big circle)
Help us to listen out for it
(cup ears)
Help us to watch out for it
(shade eyes and look around)
Thank you for all the goodness
and love that we can hear
and see.   Amen.

Second Sunday of Advent

Thought for the day

Get the road ready for the Lord!

Readings

Isaiah 11:1-10
Psalm 71:1-2, 7-8, 12-13, 17
Romans 15:4-9
Matthew 3:1-12

Aim

To think about getting ready for Jesus at Christmas.

Starter

Ready, steady, go! Give the children different tasks to do (such as running to the back wall, jumping round a chair, hopping to a leader). Having explained the task, they have to wait until you say, 'Ready, steady, go!' before they start.

Teaching

Talk about getting ready for Christmas, and all the things going on at home and in the shops. Everyone has long lists of jobs to do and cards and presents to make or buy. Show some of your own scribbled lists. How can we get ourselves ready for Christmas? Show the children an Advent calendar, with a week of windows already opened, and then open today's window. The Church calls this time before Christmas 'Advent', which is another way of saying 'coming'. We can use this time to work on something we find hard to do, like sharing our toys, going to bed when we're told to, or remembering to help at home. (Talk over the ideas with the children.) We can do this as a present to give Jesus at Christmas.

Praying

Dear Jesus,
when I open today's window
in my Advent calendar
I remember the present
I am getting ready to give you.
Please help me to do it well. Amen.

Activities

Give each child some modelling clay to make the shape of them doing what they are working at during Advent. Here are some suggestions to help the children think of their own:

- Praying every day
- Helping at home in some way
- Telling the truth
- Sharing without getting cross
- Going to bed at the right time
- Feeding/cleaning out a pet

Next week the children will be making a box to put their model in, and the week after it will be wrapped up so that all the gifts can be part of the offering at Christmas.

Notes

What are they getting ready for?

Colour this picture of John telling the crowds to get ready for Jesus

Get ready!

Colour in the red and yellow lights

For parents
Pray this with your child as you open Advent calendar windows

Dear Jesus,
when I open today's window in my Advent Calendar.
I remember the present I am getting ready to give you. Please help me to do it well!

Amen.

THIRD SUNDAY OF ADVENT

Thought for the day

Great expectations. Jesus fulfils the great statements of prophecy.

Readings

Isaiah 35:1-6, 10
Psalm 145:6-10
James 5:7-10
Matthew 11:2-11

Aim

To know that God is more wonderful than we can ever imagine, and to continue getting ready for Christmas.

Starter

Pass the parcel. Inside is a giant balloon, ready to be blown up, with the word 'God' written on it (OHP pens work well). During the game play or sing *Our God is so great* or *Think big*.

Teaching

Tell the children what it says on the balloon, and talk about how small the balloon and the word are at the moment. Is God really small and unimportant like this? No! God is the one who made the world and everything in it. (Start to blow up the balloon.)

Is that all? No! God is the one who knows and loves each of us by name. (Blow up the balloon some more.)

Is that all? What else do we know about the one true God? Collect their suggestions, making the balloon bigger with each one. Add other characteristics yourself:

- He's always ready to listen to us.
- Jesus came to show us how kind and loving he is.
- He helps us when we are sad or ill or frightened.
- He has always been alive and always will be.
- He helps us to be kind and loving and fair.

At each quality, inflate the balloon so that it is huge, and draw attention to how big God's name is now. Our God is more powerful and wonderful and loving and kind than we can ever imagine, and yet he wants to be friends with us! And he's the best friend you could ever hope to have, because he loves you, and is always there for you and will never let you down.

Praying

Our God is so big,
so strong and so mighty,
there's nothing our God cannot do! Amen.

Activities

Using the net below as a guide, cut out the shapes for the boxes from coloured paper. Help the children to assemble the boxes as shown, and place their models from last week inside, talking about what they represent and how their 'present' for Jesus is going. Encourage them in what they are doing.

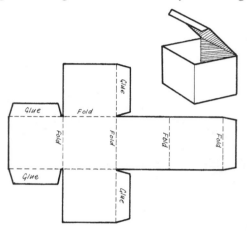

Notes

Fourth Sunday of Advent

Thought for the day

Through the willing participation of Mary and Joseph, God is poised to come among his people as their Saviour.

Readings

Isaiah 7:10-14
Psalm 23:1-6
Romans 1:1-7
Matthew 1:18-25

Aim

To see that we can help God.

Starter

Have a selection of jigsaws and other puzzles that the children can work on together, with the leader encouraging everyone to help each other.

Teaching

Draw attention to the way we all helped each other, and how good that was. Talk about what people say when they are asked to help with something. Sometimes they say things like:

'No, I don't want to.'

'No, I'm too busy.'

'No, it's too hard.'

(You could use different toys or puppets to say these things.)

Sometimes when people are asked to help they say things like:

'Yes, I'd love to.'

'Yes, I'll do that for you.'

'Yes, it sounds hard but I'll do my best.'

God needed some help for his plan to save his people. He asked Mary to help him by being Jesus' mum. He asked Joseph to help him by looking after Mary and the baby Jesus. Mary and Joseph could have said, 'No, I don't want to' (and the other refusals). The children can join in, doing the thumbs-down sign each time. But they didn't say that! They said 'Yes!' (thumbs up). So God got the help he needed, and Jesus came into the world at the first Christmas to save us and set us free.

Praying

Dear God,
when you want someone to help,
ask me.
I don't want to say 'No!' *(thumbs down)*
I want to say 'Yes!' *(thumbs up)*
Amen.

Activities

This week we are making the wrapping paper to wrap our present to God. Remind the children of their models, and print some paper with stencils or shapes dipped in paint. Wrap the box which can then be offered to God on Christmas Day. Encourage the children to keep up their resolution and offer God what they have tried their best to do. On the worksheet there is a picture to colour of Mary and Joseph going into Bethlehem.

Notes

Colour this picture

For parents to pray with your child

With love from

Dear God,
when you want
someone to help,
ask me.
I don't want to say 'NO!'
I want to say 'YES!'
Amen.

CHRISTMAS

CHRISTMAS DAY

Thought for the day

The Word of God is made flesh. In the birth of Jesus we see God expressed in human terms.

Readings

Isaiah 52:7-10
Psalm 97:1-6
Hebrews 1:1-6
John 1:1-18

Activities

Christmas Day is very much a time for all God's children to worship together.

Involve all the children in the singing and playing of carols, decorating the church, and in other ministries of welcoming, serving, collection of gifts and so on. Have nativity toys for the very young to play with, such as knitted Mary, Joseph and Jesus, sheep and shepherds. A drawing and colouring activity for today is provided.

Christmas is Jesus' birthday

First Sunday of Christmas: The Holy Family

Thought for the day

Jesus, the expression of God's love, lives as a vulnerable boy in the real and dangerous world we all inhabit.

Readings

Ecclesiasticus* 3:2-6, 12-14 (* also called Sirach)
Psalm 127:1-5
Colossians 3:12-21
Matthew 2:13-15, 19-23

Aim

To know that Joseph worked with God to keep his family safe.

Starter

Sharks! Scatter some random shapes of newspaper around on the floor to be islands. When the music is playing everyone swims around in the sea enjoying themselves. When the music stops, and the leader calls out, 'Watch out – sharks about!' everyone swims to the safety of an island and stands there until the all-clear, when the music starts again.

Teaching

Talk about how we had to go where it was safe, when we were in danger from the sharks. People who love us look after us to make sure we are safe. We look after those we love (both people and animals) to make sure they are safe. God loves to see us all looking after one another like this, because he loves all of us.

Let the children give some examples of ways people look after them to make sure they are safe, such as marking a yellow line on the station platform to stand behind, belting us up in the car, and helping us to cross the road. When people check that we have warm clothes to go out in, and that we are getting enough sleep, or when they tell us off for doing something dangerous, they are showing their love by looking after us!

God made sure Jesus was as safe as possible in the dangerous world by having Joseph and Mary to look after him. How would they do that? As well as all the usual ways, they had some big dangers to cope with. One night, God told Joseph that King Herod was out looking for Jesus so that he could kill him. So Joseph got up in the middle of the night. He packed up some food and clothes and strapped them on the sleepy donkey. Then he woke Mary up.

'Mary! Wake up! Jesus is in danger. We'll have to leave Bethlehem and go where he will be safe. Come on!'

Mary and Joseph crept around as quietly as they could so that no one would hear them going. They wrapped Jesus up and hoped he wouldn't wake up and cry. They walked through the dark streets, very frightened, and when they left the town they walked on and on through the hills. Jesus woke up and still they walked on, for several days, until at last they got to Egypt, where they knew they were safe. King Herod couldn't come after Jesus there. They only went back home when they heard that King Herod had died.

Praying

God bless my family.
Look after us all.
Help us look after each other.
In life and death
keep us safe for ever. Amen.

Activities

Using upturned bowls and a large cloth, sheet or towel, make a model of the landscape. Using a cut-out picture of Mary, Jesus and Joseph, based on the one on the worksheet, all the children can have a go at taking the family to safety.

Notes

Colour in Mary, Joseph, Jesus and the donkey

Cut out and stick on thin card

Fold so they stand up

Cut

Quick! Give her an umbrella before she gets soaked

Quick! Give him a helmet before he falls on the ground!

Shh!

walk?

eat a crisp?

put on your coat?

How quietly can you . . .

For parents to pray with your child

God bless my family.
Look after us all.
Help us look after each other.
In life and death keep us safe for ever.   Amen.

Cut

Second Sunday of Christmas

Thought for the day

The grace and truth revealed in Jesus show God's freely given love; through Jesus, God pours out his blessings on us and gives us real freedom.

Readings

Ecclesiasticus 24:1-4, 12-16
Psalm 147:12-15, 19-20
Ephesians 1:3-6, 15-18
John 1:1-18

Aim

To know that Jesus is God saying, 'I love you!'

Starter

Show me you're happy! Sit everyone in a circle. Just using their faces, ask them to show you they're happy/sad/in pain/excited/tired, etc.

Teaching

They were so good at showing those feelings that you could tell what they were thinking inside! Our bodies are very useful for helping us tell people how we feel. How can you show your mum, dad, grandma or baby cousin that you love them? How do they show that they love you?

Jesus is God saying, 'I love you!' No one has ever seen God while they are alive on earth. He can't be seen. But in Jesus, being born as a baby, growing up and walking around as an adult, we can see God's love.

Praying

Thank you, Jesus,
for being born
into our world.
Thank you for showing us
God's love. Amen.

Activities

On the worksheet there is a dot-to-dot picture to complete, so that they can see something clearly which they couldn't see before. Have lots of pieces of Christmas wrapping paper, pieces of ribbon and milk-bottle tops to stick on coloured paper to make the suggested collage.

I love you!

Make a lovely picture by sticking on all sorts of bits and pieces
Give it to someone you love

Join the dots to see clearly something very lovable

Give it a name – your helper will write it in for you

For parents to pray with your child

Thank you, Jesus, for being born into our world. Thank you for showing us God's love.   Amen.

THE EPIPHANY OF THE LORD

Thought for the day

Jesus, the hope of the nations, is shown to the world.

Readings

Isaiah 60:1-6
Psalm 71:1-2, 7-8, 10-13
Ephesians 3:2-3a, 5-6
Matthew 2:1-12

Aim

To become familiar with the story of the wise men finding Jesus.

Starter

Play 'pass the parcel'. At the different layers have old bus and train tickets. The prize at the end is a star-shaped biscuit.

Teaching

Tell the children that today we are going to hear about a journey. It isn't a bus journey or a car journey or a train journey. This is a camel journey. (All pack your bags and get on your camels.) We are very wise people, but we don't know where we are going. We are looking for a baby king. And we are packing presents for him. (Pack gold, frankincense and myrrh.) Produce a star on a stick as you explain how a special star has started shining in the sky and we are sure it will lead us to the baby king. Lead off behind the star, riding your camels, and pretending to go over high mountains, through water, stopping for the night, and going to sleep and so on. At last you reach the town of Bethlehem (stick up a sign) where you find the baby king with his mum and dad. (Have a large picture, or one of the cribs made before Christmas.) We all get off our camels and give the baby our presents. The baby's name is Jesus and we have found him at last!

Praying

This is a prayer the wise men might have said. We have all been invited to find Jesus as well, so we can say it with them.

Thank you, Jesus,
for inviting me
to come and look for you.
I am glad I have found you! Amen.

Activities

To emphasise that the journey of the wise men was probably a hard one, there is a maze to help the wise men find their way to Bethlehem. The star-making activity will need star templates, and ready-cut card for the younger children.

Notes

You will need

glue

glitter

scissors

crayons

Frankincense

Gold

Myrrh

Please
let me see
the right
way to go,
Jesus. Amen.

For parents
You may like to have the star your
child has made put in the car or by
the front door

THE BAPTISM OF THE LORD

Thought for the day

As Jesus is baptised, the Spirit of God rests visibly on him, marking him out as the One who will save his people.

Readings

Isaiah 42:1-4, 6-7
Psalm 28:1-4, 9-10
Acts 10:34-38
Matthew 3:13-17

Aim

To know that Jesus was baptised in the river Jordan.

Starter

Water play. Protect the floor and have some bowls of water and plastic bowls, funnels and tubes for the children to play with.

Teaching

Talk about all the things we could do with the water. Water is so useful to us because it makes us clean when we're dirty, we can drink it and cook with it, and we can paddle and swim in it too. Show the children some pictures of seas and oceans, rivers and ponds.

We have to be very careful with water because we can't breathe in it. We can drown in it.

That makes water a very good way of explaining what happens at Baptism: we drown to everything evil, and come up with our sins all washed clean away by God.

Talk about any Baptisms in their families that they remember – or even their own.

When Jesus walked into the water in the River Jordan, he asked to be baptised as well. So John poured the water over him, and when he came up out of the water, God's Spirit, like a dove, flew out of heaven and rested on him. God said, 'This is my Son. I love him very much.' When *we* are baptised, God is saying, 'This is my daughter, Eleanor; this is my son, Richard. And I love them very much!'

Praying

Dear God,
I'm glad you love me.
I like being one of your children! Amen.

Activities

Use water added to paint and make some bright pictures to thank God for water. Let the children watch the paint-making, or use blocks of water-colour so they need to keep dipping their brushes in the water to clean them and to make the picture beautiful.

Notes

24

water + paint powder = paint!

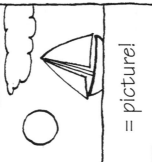

= picture!

water + paint + brush

For parents
Draw your child's attention
to all the times we use and
need water this week

Dear God,
I'm glad you love me
I like being one of
your children!
Amen.

Thank you, God, for water!

LENT

FIRST SUNDAY
OF LENT

Thought for the day

Jesus knows all about temptation; and he can deal with our sin.

Readings

Genesis 2:7-9; 3:1-7
Psalm 50:3-6, 12-14, 17
Romans 5:12-19
Matthew 4:1-11

Aim

To know the Adam and Eve temptation story.

Starter

Put out chairs all over the room, with a cross on the chair in the middle. Play musical chairs, telling everyone first that they mustn't sit on the chair in the middle, even if it's the only chair left.

Teaching

Talk about how well they managed/how hard they found it to keep the rule during the game. Today we are going to hear about Adam and Eve who had a rule to keep.

Tell the story either from a children's adapted version, in your own words based on the biblical account, or from a suitable Bible translation (see 'Recommended Bibles', page 7). Accompany the words with pictures, either from the book you are using or using the carpet tiles and cut-outs of trees, Adam, Eve and the snake. In this case the children can help by placing the trees and fruit on the background. At the point where they are told not to eat from the tree in the middle of the garden, place a cross on the centre tree.

Praying

Jesus, you want us to be loving each day
and we say, 'OK!'
Jesus, you want us to do as you say
and we say, 'OK!'

Activities

On the activity sheet they can count all the fruit Adam and Eve are allowed to eat, and there are outlines for trees and characters to make into a model. Each child will need a flat piece of card for this, and either green paper or green chopped wool to stick on it. If you prefer, you can make one big communal model.

Notes

26

Cut out and colour in

Fold and stick to base

Cut out and colour in

Fold and stick to base

Fold and stick to base

Fold and stick to base

Cut out and colour in

Jesus, you want us to be loving each day and we say OK!

Jesus, you want us to do as you say and we say OK!

For parents to pray with your child

How many apples can they eat?

Adam and Eve can eat all the fruit except from the middle tree

Second Sunday of Lent

Thought for the day

The disciples witness the glory of God revealed in Jesus. It is a glimpse of the glory which will be the great hope for all nations of the world.

Readings

Genesis 12:1-4a
Psalm 32
2 Timothy 1:8-10
Matthew 17:1-9

Aim

To think about how wonderful God is.

Starter

Sit in a circle and pass round something natural and beautiful, such as a shell, a flower or a pineapple. Each person says one thing they notice about it. This encourages very careful observation and enjoyment of detail. The leader can draw attention to what a lot of things we managed to notice in this one bit of God's world.

Teaching

Have some quiet, gentle music playing, and ask the children to lie down with their eyes closed as you take them on a lovely journey.

Imagine you find a door in a wall. There is a handle on the door and you open it. On the other side of the door the sun is shining and the sky is blue. There are birds singing. You feel warm and happy. You run in bare feet over the springy grass through the daisies and buttercups, and a bright blue butterfly flies beside you. You can hear the sound of the sea, swishing gently on the sand. Now you can see the water, and you walk over the sand to the edge of the cool water and stand in it, with the water trickling over your feet. A boat is being rowed towards you and inside is someone you know and love and trust. Perhaps it's your mum or dad. Perhaps it's Jesus. They help you into the boat and you sit there safely and happily, looking at the clear water and at the hills in the distance, enjoying the lapping sound of the water against the boat. The boat comes back to the sandy beach, and you climb out and walk back over the soft sand, over the springy green grass with the daisies and buttercups, till you get back to the door in the wall. You go through the door and close it behind you, feeling all happy and rested. The door has your own name

written on it and you can go back there whenever you want.

Tell the children that when the music stops they can open their eyes and sit up, and gradually fade the music out so this is not a jolt for them. If the children want to talk about their journey allow a little time for this; it very much depends on the personality of the child.

Talk about the way God has made us a beautiful place to live in and the way he loves us. With God we can feel safe and happy, because there is absolutely nothing nasty or frightening about God. He is completely good and right and true and fair.

Praying

Go straight into the praying after the teaching, making a beautiful focus for the children using shells or flowers and candles, perhaps with a globe.

Holy, holy, holy Lord,
God of power and might,
heaven and earth
are full of your glory!

Activities

The children will need white candles or white wax crayons to draw pictures with. They then paint with water-based colours over their drawings so that they see clearly what they have already drawn, rather as we have been noticing God's glory in the starter and the teaching. There are also examples of God's glory to colour on the worksheet.

Notes

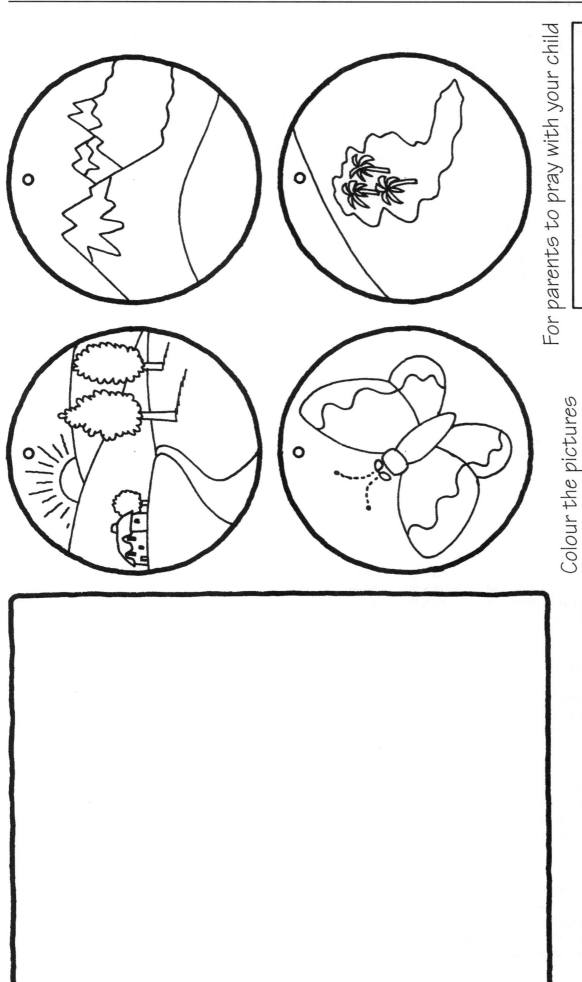

For parents to pray with your child

Holy, holy, holy Lord,
God of power and might,
heaven and earth
are full of your glory!

Colour the pictures
They show God's glory
Tie cotton to them
and hang them up

Draw a picture with a white candle or white
wax crayon. Paint over the drawing with
colours and see your drawing show up

THIRD SUNDAY OF LENT

Thought for the day

God both knows us completely and loves us completely; meeting us where we are, he provides us with living water, to satisfy all our needs.

Readings

Exodus 17:3-7
Psalm 94:1-2, 6-9
Romans 5:1-2, 5-8
John 4:5-42

Aim

To know that God can supply our needs.

Starter

Give the children little boxes to fill with little things. Either take them outside to do this (if you have a convenient church garden) or scatter suitable objects around the room so that they can go round collecting them.

Teaching

Introduce two or three puppets or character toys who are trying to use things that don't work very well and are disappointing as they keep letting them down. You can have items that are particularly relevant to your group, but here are some general ideas to start your thinking off: a pencil or crayon which keeps breaking, a leaky bucket, gloves with holes in so your hands get cold, a thin plastic knife and fork which snap, and water that tastes horrid.

Jesus is like a good bucket or like a glove/pencil that really works. (Let the puppets try these and be suitably delighted.) Jesus is like good-tasting, clear water which really quenches our thirst. We can trust Jesus to satisfy our deepest needs.

Praying

My lovely God,
thank you for supplying all our needs,
like a fresh, clear spring of water
which never runs dry. Amen.

Activities

On the sheet there are pictures to colour which encourage discussion about the way water can supply different needs, and a 'spot the loving' picture which shows love supplying other needs. The children can also make a water wheel. Prepare for this by cutting a yoghurt or margarine tub as shown below. The children can fix the plastic 'blades' in the slots and thread the wheel on a pencil. When held under a running tap the wheel will turn.

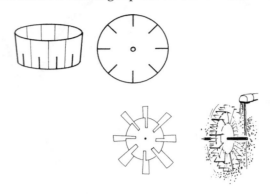

Notes

How does water give us what we need?

Spot the loving

For parents to pray with your child

My lovely God,
thank you for supplying
all our needs, like a fresh,
clear spring of water
which never runs dry.
Amen.

Fourth Sunday of Lent

Thought for the day

Jesus gives sight to the man born blind and exposes the blindness of those who claim to see.

Readings

1 Samuel 16:1, 6-7, 10-13
Psalm 22
Ephesians 5:8-14
John 9:1-41

Aim

To praise God for all the things we can see.

Starter

Pass round a 'feelie bag' in which there are two or three things. Each child feels what is inside, and once everyone has had a go, you can share ideas about what is in the bag. Tip the contents out to see how our guesses match up with the reality.

Teaching

Cover several hoops in different colours, laid down on matching coloured paper, and bring an assortment of objects, both natural and manufactured, both tiny and large, and some pictures which the children can sort according to colour, so that you end up with each hoop being a colour display. You could get each child or small group to work on a particular colour. Wind some rainbow colours of ribbon or crepe paper between the hoops.

Admire the displays, and ask everyone to shut their eyes, then open them again. Our eyes give us so much fun; God has made so many lovely things to see, and with our eyes we can see them and enjoy them.

Praying

Red and yellow, green and blue,
we are giving thanks to you!
Orange, purple, pink and grey,
your colours brighten up the day.
Thank you for them all –
my favourite is (*everyone shouts out their favourite*)

Activities

There is a pattern to colour in their favourite colours using mosaic (squares of coloured paper cut from old greetings cards and sorted into colour bowls) and a picture of some red things, some blue things and some green things, so the children will need these colours of crayons.

Notes

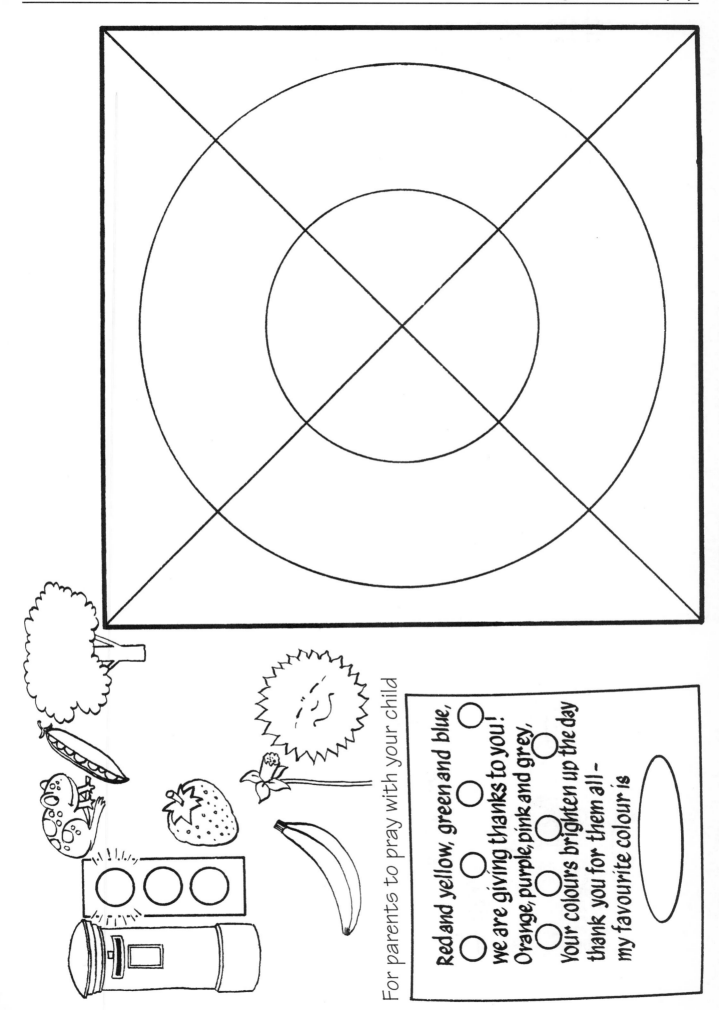

For parents to pray with your child

Red and yellow, green and blue,
we are giving thanks to you!
Orange, purple, pink and grey.
Your colours brighten up the day
thank you for them all –
my favourite colour is

FIFTH SUNDAY OF LENT

Thought for the day

Jesus is the resurrection and the life. He can transform death and despair, in any form, into life and hope.

Readings

Ezekiel 37:12-14
Psalm 129
Romans 8:8-11
John 11:1-45

Aim

To know that God gives life and hope.

Starter

Inflatable toys to blow up and then play with.

Teaching

Get all the children breathing in and out while they hold their ribs, so they can feel the air going in and out. Talk about the way we breathed air into the inflatable toys so that we were able to play with them. Just as our bodies need air, so our spirits need God's Spirit. God gives us life and God gives us hope.

Now spread carpet tiles, bath towels or a sheet on the floor, and use the pictures below to make larger cut-outs from thin card. Gather the children around the edge and move the figures as you tell the story of Lazarus being brought back to life again.

Praying

God be in my head and in my thinking.
(hold head with both hands)
God be in my hands and in my doing.
(hold out hands)
God be in my heart and in my loving. Amen.
(hands on heart, then arms and hands stretched out)

Activities

On the sheet there are some pictures of people and animals in very tricky situations. The children can draw in something that brings them hope. Also the Lazarus story can be made into a book to take home and read. The children will need coloured mounting paper already cut to size, a hole punch and a length of wool, or a stapler.

Notes

LAZARUS is alive!

Colour the pictures in order, cut them out and make a book to read like this

For parents to pray with your child

God be in my head and in my thinking (Hold head with both hands)
God be in my hands and in my doing (Hold out hands)
God be in my heart and in my loving (Hands on heart, then arms and hands stretched out)
Amen.

HELP!

Can you help? The cat is stuck!

HELP!

No water! Can you help?

HELP!

Hungry! Can you help?

HOLY WEEK

PALM (PASSION) SUNDAY

Thought for the day

Jesus rides into Jerusalem cheered by the crowds. Days later, crowds will be clamouring for his death.

Readings

Liturgy of the Palms:
Matthew 21:1-11

Liturgy of the Passion:
Isaiah 50:4-7
Psalm 21:8-9, 17-20, 23-24
Philippians 2:6-11
Matthew 26:14-27:66 or Matthew 27:11-54

Aim

To welcome Jesus, the king on a donkey.

Starter

If your church has a Palm Sunday procession, then the children will be joining in with this. Provide them with palms to wave, and ask for one of the hymns to be one the children can cope with, such as *Hosanna, hosanna!* or *Rejoice in the Lord always*. If the church doesn't organise a procession, there might be a special one for the children.

Teaching

Tell the children the story of Jesus coming into Jerusalem on a donkey, either using your own words based on a careful reading of the Bible text, or one of the versions available for young children. As you tell the story, get the children to join in with all the actions, such as miming the untying of the donkey and leading it to Jesus, the waving of palm branches and laying coats on the road, and shouting 'Hooray for Jesus!'

Praying

Clip, clop, clip, clop!
Hosanna! Hosanna!
Hooray for Jesus,
the king on a donkey!
Hosanna! Hosanna!
Clip, clop, clip, clop!

Activities

Use the pattern on the sheet to make palm branches from green paper. There is also a road drawn on the sheet and a donkey to cut out and lead along the road into Jerusalem. Children will need assistance with the cutting. For very young children have the donkey already cut out.

Notes

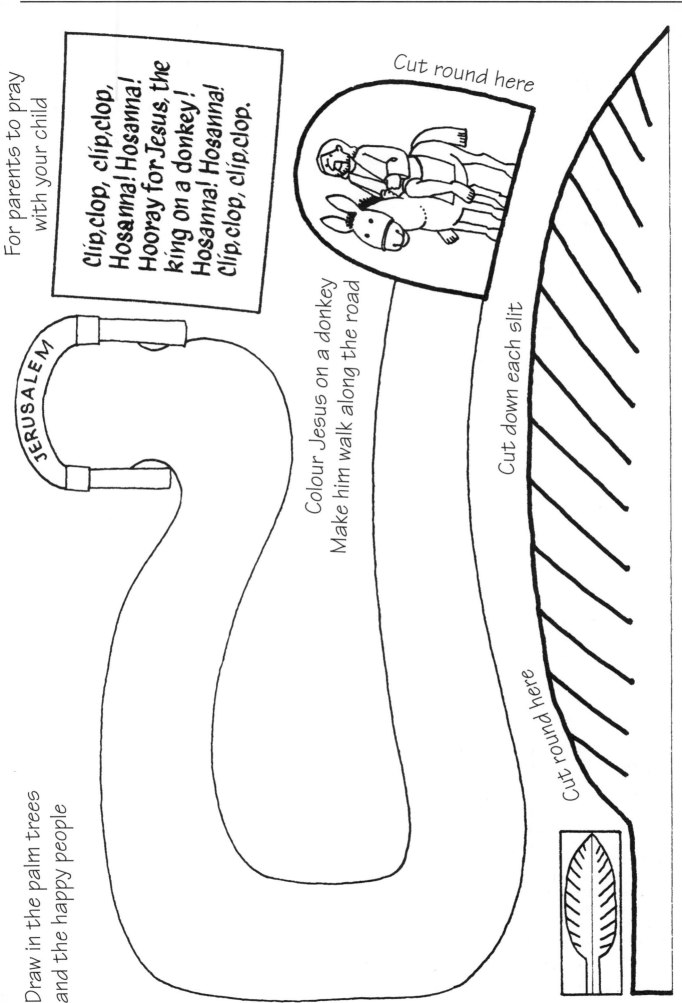

For parents to pray with your child

Clip,clop, clip,clop, Hosanna! Hosanna! Hooray for Jesus, the king on a donkey! Hosanna! Hosanna! Clip,clop, clip,clop.

Cut round here

JERUSALEM

Colour Jesus on a donkey
Make him walk along the road

Cut down each slit

Cut round here

Put the side on folded green paper

Draw in the palm trees and the happy people

EASTER

EASTER DAY

If possible, it is recommended that the children and young people are in church with the other age groups today. Use and adapt some of the all-age ideas from the *Living Water* Complete Resource Book, and involve the young people in some of the music and in the cleaning and decorating of the church.

Thought for the day

It is true. Jesus is alive for all time. The Lord of life cannot be held by death. God's victory over sin and death means that new life for us is a reality.

Readings

Acts 10:34-43
Psalm 117:1-2, 16-17, 22-23
Colossians 3:1-4
John 20:1-9

Aim

To enjoy celebrating that Jesus is alive.

Starter

Have an Easter egg hunt, preferably outside if this is safe and practical.

Teaching

Using a blackboard and chalks, draw the story as you tell it. Please don't be put off and think you won't be able to do it as you can't draw! Young children will be fascinated by the story being drawn, however simple the drawing, and will be quite happy to imagine the bits your drawing leaves out. So do try it!

Start with the green hill outside the city of Jerusalem with the three crosses on it, and tell the children that this is where Jesus had been killed on Good Friday. Now draw in a garden with a cave, and tell the children how Jesus' friends sadly took his body down from the cross and put it in a cave. They rolled a huge heavy stone across the front of the cave to shut it. (Draw in the stone.) The next day was the day when everyone rested. Then on Sunday (which is the same day as today), when it was very early and not even light yet, some of Jesus' friends came to the garden. They wanted to put some sweet-smelling ointment on Jesus' body. (Draw them in at the cave.)

They had been wondering who they could get to move the heavy stone for them, but they were in for a big surprise. When they got to the cave they found that the stone had been rolled away! (Rub it out and draw it in at the side of the cave.) Sitting on the stone was an angel, all full of light. (Draw in the angel.) The angel told them that Jesus wasn't dead any more but had risen from the dead and was alive! The women were very surprised. (Make O shapes for their mouths.) Then suddenly they realised that Jesus was standing there, right next to them! (Draw him in.) The women were very happy to see Jesus. (Change their mouths into smiles.) They went back to tell Jesus' other friends that he was alive, not just for now, but for ever. (Change their legs to be running.)

Praying

Jesus, you died for me
   (arms out like a cross)
Jesus, you came to life for me!
   (arms up)
Jesus, you are alive for ever and ever and ever!
   (clap, clap, clap during the 'evers'.)

Activities

On the sheet they can follow the footsteps of the women to find where they have gone, and draw in the flowers in the garden. They can also decorate a hard-boiled egg with felt-tip pens or paints.

Notes

38

New Life

Paint a hard-boiled egg!

Jesus, you died for me
(arms out like a cross)
Jesus, you came to life for
me (arms up)
Jesus, you are alive for ever
and ever and ever!
(clap, clap, clap during the 'evers')
Amen.

Where did those women go?

For parents to pray with your child

SECOND SUNDAY OF EASTER

Thought for the day

Through the risen Jesus we have a living hope which will never spoil or fade.

Readings

Acts 2:42-47
Psalm 117:2-4, 13-15, 22-24
1 Peter 1:3-9
John 20:19-31

Aim

To know we can sometimes trust what we can't see.

Starter

With the very young play a 'peep-bo' game. With the older children play 'hunt the trainer', telling the children first that there is a trainer somewhere in the room, even though they can't see it yet.

Teaching

Was the trainer there all the time? Yes it was, even though we couldn't see it. We can't see the air all around us but we know it's there because we are alive, breathing the air in and out of our bodies. We can't see Jesus, but we know he is here with us and he can see us.

Jesus can hear us, too, so we can talk to him. Who has some good news to tell Jesus and the rest of us? Have a time of sharing the children's news, in Jesus' company. Jesus loves us, so we can trust him with the things that make us sad as well as the happy things. Have a time of telling Jesus about some of the things that make us sad. After each one lead the children to ask for Jesus' help, either to comfort the person or animal, or simply to be there with them and bring some good thing out of a bad time.

What shall we sing to Jesus? All sing a favourite song (it doesn't have to be a hymn), singing our best, just for Jesus, who is listening, and loves to be with us.

Praying

Who cares if I can't see you?
(shrug shoulders with hands open)
I certainly know that you're here!
(nod)
Who cares if I can't touch you?
(shrug shoulders with hands open)
I certainly know that you're here!
(nod)
You love me.
(hands on heart)
You listen to me.
(touch ears)
You see me
(point to eyes)
and you talk to me.
(fingers to mouth then out from it)
So who cares if I can't see you?
(shrug shoulders with hands open)
I certainly know you're here!
(nod)

Activities

The children will need a piece of white candle each. On the sheet they can draw Jesus in wax in the picture of the Treasure Seekers in their group, and then with a light watercolour wash, paint over the picture so that Jesus can be seen. Protect the children's clothing before they start.

Notes

Jesus with the Treasure Seekers group

We can't see Jesus, but we know he is here with us. He likes us

You will need 👁 and 🖊 🎨

For parents to pray with your child

Who cares if I can't see you?
(shrug shoulders with hands open)
I certainly know that you're here! (nod)
Who cares if I can't touch you?
(shrug shoulders with hands open)
I certainly know that you're here! (nod)
You love me (hands on heart)
You listen to me (touch ears)
You see me (point to eyes)
and you talk to me.
(fingers to mouth, then out from it)
So who cares if I can't see you?
(shrug shoulders with hands open)
I certainly know you're here! (nod)

THIRD SUNDAY OF EASTER

Thought for the day

Jesus explains the scriptures and is recognised in the breaking of bread.

Readings

Acts 2:14a, 22-28
Psalm 15:1-2, 5, 7-11
1 Peter 1:17-21
Luke 24:13-35

Aim

To know that the risen Jesus walks beside us through life.

Starter

Play with various puzzle games such as jigsaws and shape puzzles. Or play Kim's game, where you set out a number of different objects on a tray and let everyone look at them for a while. Then cover the tray and see how many things they can remember. The children are having to work things out, and experience that this isn't always easy.

Teaching

Set up a length of lining paper on which you have drawn Jerusalem at one end (with the green hill, the crosses and the cave in the garden) and the little town of Emmaus at the other end. Draw a winding road going between the two places. Use this as you recap on the events leading up to the Resurrection and also for today's teaching.

Remind the children that on the first Easter Day – Easter is the day we all have Easter eggs – Jesus came to life. He had died on the cross on the Friday and his friends had put his body in the cave and fixed a great big stone like a door to shut the cave. And early on the Sunday morning, when the women came to the garden, what did they find? They found the stone rolled away and Jesus' dead body wasn't in the cave because he wasn't dead any more – he was alive! Alive so that he would never die again. (They will be able to help you with the story. It will be interesting to discover which details they remember best!)

Today we are going to hear about two friends of Jesus who lived about seven miles from Jerusalem. On that same day they were walking home. (Have two toys to walk along the road, starting at Jerusalem.) They were very sad because their dear friend Jesus had died. Just then another traveller caught them up and they all said hello. The stranger said to them, 'Why are you both looking so sad?'

'Haven't you heard?' they said, 'We're sad because Jesus is dead. He was so kind and good, and he told us good stories to teach us about God, and he made people better, and we hoped he would be the leader of our country. But he was put to death on a cross, even though he hadn't done anything wrong at all. Some women said they saw him alive this morning but we don't know whether to believe their story. It's all a big puzzle, and we don't understand it at all.'

As the three of them walked along, the stranger talked. He helped them to understand the things they were puzzling over. He helped them understand that Jesus had said he would have to go through pain and death, but that he would come through that to be alive again. The two friends started to feel a bit happier and a bit more hopeful.

Just then they got near their town. The stranger began to wave goodbye. 'Oh, don't go!' said the friends. 'Come in and have something to eat with us.' So he did. At the meal, the stranger took some bread and thanked God for it. Then he broke it . . . and suddenly the two friends knew exactly who the stranger was! (Can the children guess?) Yes, it was Jesus, and he really was alive!

Praying

Walk with me, Jesus,
today and every day.
I want to walk with you, Jesus,
right through my life! Amen.

Activities

On the sheet there is the road for the children to make the two friends walk down with Jesus. To make the friends stand up, stick them on card as shown. Then they can tell the story again, and to their parents in the week.

Notes

Emmaus

To make the figures stand up

Two friends

Jesus

Jerusalem

For parents to pray with your child

Walk with me, Jesus, today and every day. I want to walk with you, Jesus, right through my life! Amen.

Fourth Sunday of Easter

Thought for the day

Jesus, the Good Shepherd, has come so that we may have life in rich abundance.

Readings

Acts 2:14, 36-41
Psalm 22:1-6
1 Peter 2:20-28
John 10:1-10

Aim

To know that Jesus is like a good shepherd who loves his sheep and lambs.

Starter

Have hidden around enough toy lambs and sheep (or pictures of them) for each child to find one. Lay down a mat which can be a sheep pen and tell the children that there are lots of sheep all over the hill-side which need bringing home for the night. Send the children off to collect one sheep each and put them safely in the sheepfold.

Teaching

Praise them for being such good shepherds when they brought in all the sheep, and talk with them about why sheep need to be safely looked after at night if there are wolves and foxes and bears around. (They may have pets which need putting away at night for the same reason.)

Talk about the way shepherds are people who look after sheep. How do we look after our pets? Bring out the need to care for them every day and night, and not just when we feel like it.

Show them a picture of Jesus as the Good Shepherd and explain that Jesus looks after us like a good shepherd looks after his sheep – so we are like Jesus' lambs, and he is our shepherd, taking great care of us all the time. He gives us sleep when we are tired, food and drink when we are hungry and thirsty, and other lambs to play with.

Praying

Dear Jesus, you are my shepherd
and I am one of your lambs.
Thank you for loving me
and looking after me. Amen.

Activities

The children can make a sheep mask to wear, based on the shape drawn on the sheet. They will also need some glue and chopped white wool. There is a picture to which the children can add other sheep and lambs, either by drawing, or by sticking on pre-cut shapes.

Notes

FIFTH SUNDAY OF EASTER

Thought for the day

Jesus is the Way, the Truth and the Life, through whom we can come into the presence of God for ever.

Readings

Acts 6:1-7
Psalm 32:1-2, 4-5, 18-19
1 Peter 2:4-9
John 14:1-12

Aim

To know that Jesus is like a road that leads us to heaven.

Starter

Gather a collection of vehicles to play with – model cars and lorries, and a sit-and-ride or two. Have a time of car play, either all over the floor, or on a road mat if you have one.

Teaching

Take the children to look at a road, either looking through a window, or going outside (in which case ensure that the children are holding hands with adults or some of the older children, and are well supervised). Talk about what the road looks like, and where it is going. Then come back inside.

Roads are very useful things. You can drive along a road easily without bumping into trees or falling into the sea, because the road is a clear way. A road will take you straight to the shops, or the park, or to church. It stops you getting lost in the mountains if you keep on the clear roadway.

Jesus said he was like a clear roadway that we can travel on to heaven. The Jesus road is clear and strong. If we travel the Jesus Way through life, then, like the best roads, it will take us safely home, at the end of our life here, to live with God for ever in heaven.

Mark a road with chairs, and all walk along it, repeating the prayer in time to the marching.

Praying

Left, right, left, right,
Jesus you're the Way!
Left, right, left, right,
we'll walk your Way today!

Activities

On the sheet they can try drawing roads from one place to another, and there is a 'Jesus knows the way!' badge to colour. It can then be stuck on to pre-cut thin card, and attached to their clothes with a piece of double-sided sticky tape.

Notes

Go from the house to the school

Go from the shop to the church

Go from the school to the park

Jesus knows the Way!

For parents to pray with your child

Left, right, left, right,
Jesus, you're the Way!
Left, right, left, right,
we'll walk your Way
TODAY!

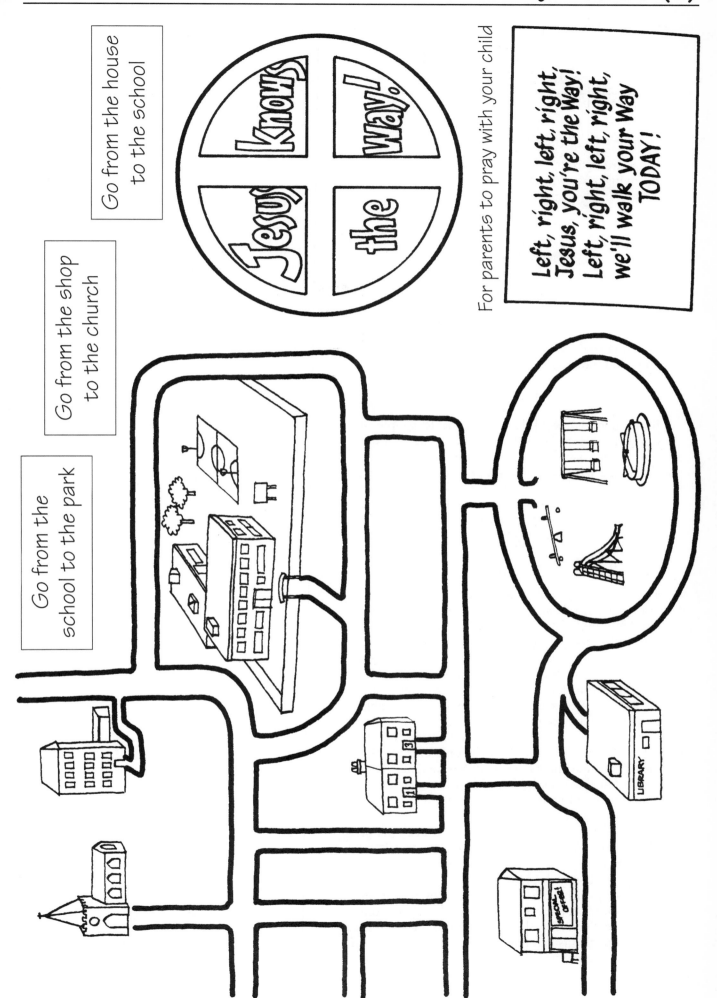

SIXTH SUNDAY OF EASTER

Thought for the day

The Spirit of truth, given to us, enables us to discern the living, risen Christ.

Readings

Acts 8:5-8, 14-17
Psalm 65:1-7, 16, 20
1 Peter 3:15-18
John 14:15-21

Aim

To know that we can go on getting to know God more and more till we are old.

Starter

Bring along some clothes belonging to people of different ages to be sorted in order. They should range from baby clothes and nappies to walking sticks and warm sensible slippers, taking in some fashionable items for teenagers and smart office clothing along the way. Have some fun deciding which age would wear them, and end with them in a line, from youngest to oldest.

Teaching

Those clothes told us a story. They told us that we don't stay the same as when we are born. We get older and bigger and grow up. As we grow up we learn all sorts of things. Like what, for instance? Share their ideas of what they think we learn. As we grow we also get better at doing things, like moving about, talking, singing, eating tidily and dressing ourselves. What would they like to be able to do which they can't quite manage yet?

Another important thing we do as we grow up is to make friends. We get to know people and we like them. We get to know them a bit more and like them even better. Friendship grows like we do, as we spend time with our friends and talk, and play together. Friendship grows as we help one another, too.

It's just the same with our friend, Jesus. First of all we don't know him very well. People tell us about him and we think he sounds nice. But we make friends with him by spending time with him and talking and playing with him. Bit by bit we get to know Jesus better, and find that we love him more and more. Even now, the leaders are still getting to know him. Think of some elderly Christians they know at church, or invite one or two along. Even these people are still finding they're getting to know Jesus and love him more.

So as you grow, and grow out of your clothes, right through until you are so old that your hair is white and you need a stick to walk with, you and Jesus can go on being friends, and he'll show you more and more of what he is like, all through your life.

Praying

When I was a baby,
  (crouch down small)
I know you loved me, Jesus.
Now I am as tall as this,
  (stand at normal height)
I know you as my friend.
When I am as tall as this, or this, or this, or this,
  (measure with hand at levels above head)
or even when I walk like this,
  (pretend to walk with stick as an old person)
we'll still be best of friends.

Activities

On the sheet there are people to put in order of age. Then they can count the friends of Jesus, so they realise that they all are his friends, whatever the age. There is also an illustration of a height chart to make. Each child will need a pre-cut length of paper which has the heights marked on it, and the words: 'Jesus' friends grow'. The children decorate the chart with paints or stickers.

Notes

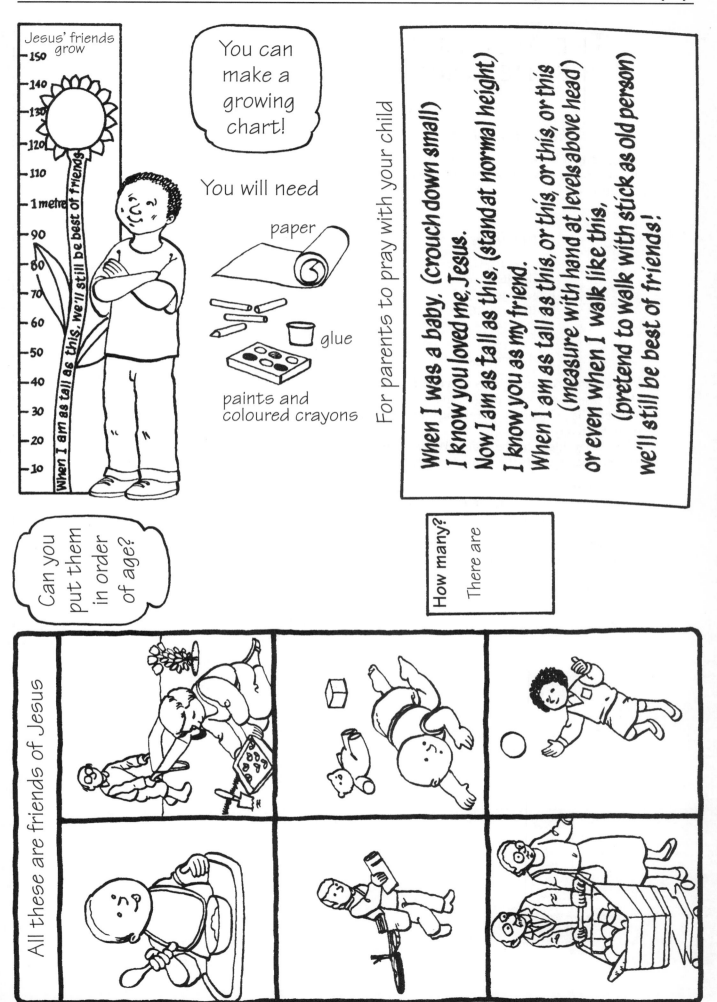

THE ASCENSION OF THE LORD

Thought for the day

Having bought back our freedom with the giving of his life, Jesus enters into the full glory to which he is entitled.

Readings

Acts 1:1-11
Psalm 46:2-3, 6-9
Ephesians 1:17-23
Matthew 28:16-20

Activities

It is likely that Ascension Day services for schools will not need a separate programme for children. However, I have included a drawing and colouring activity for today.

The all-age ideas in the *Living Water* Complete Resource Book include the following suggestions.

- Any artwork or writing that the children have done on what the Ascension is about can be displayed around the building.

- Have a beautiful helium balloon at the ready. Write on it an Ascension message that the children would like to send. After the service two representative children can let the balloon float away.

SEVENTH SUNDAY OF EASTER

Thought for the day

God's glory is often revealed in the context of suffering and failure in the world's eyes.

Readings

Acts 1:12-14
Psalm 26:1, 4, 7-8
1 Peter 4:13-16
John 17:1-11

Aim

To know that Jesus went back into heaven.

Starter

Guess who's coming through the door. Introduce a number of different toys and then bundle them all behind a 'door'. The leader says, 'Guess who's coming through the door', and the children all shout out who they think it is. Vary the length of time they shout, before making one of the toys walk through the door. Repeat until all the toys are outside. Sometimes a toy can go back behind the door again and come out for a second time.

Teaching

What a lot of coming and going there was in that game! Remind the children that since Easter (which will seem a very long time ago) when we remembered Jesus coming to life again, we've had stories of him coming and going, meeting his friends. Sometimes they could see Jesus and sometimes they couldn't.

It went on like that for about the same time as from Easter Day to now. Jesus' friends were starting to understand that Jesus could still be with them, even if they couldn't see him.

One day Jesus was with them all outside. It was time for Jesus to say goodbye to his friends and go back to heaven. 'Don't worry,' he said, 'I won't leave you on your own. I will ask my Father and he will send you the Holy Spirit to give you strength and comfort. It means that I shall be with you all the time, wherever you go.' Then, as they watched, Jesus was lifted up from the ground and a cloud hid him from them. They knew they would not see him again in the same way, but they knew he would be with them, loving them and looking after them.

Like those friends of Jesus, we can't see him with our eyes, but we know he is just as real and alive now as he was then. And when we ask him to be near us and help us he is right there, straight away.

Praying

Jesus, you were born as a baby
   (rock baby in arms)
you worked as a carpenter, sawing the wood.
   (saw wood)
You died on a cross and you rose again.
   (arms out, then jump and clap hands)
You are loving and kind and good.
   (put up fingers, counting to three)
In heaven and on earth your glory shines.
   *(point up and down,
   then trace big circle with fingers stretched out)*
You are loving and kind and good.
   (count on fingers again)

Activities

On the sheet there is a picture of the Ascension for the children to add to and colour, or they can complete the picture as a mosaic. For this, pre-cut pieces of different colours from old greetings cards, and place the different colours in separate tubs. The children stick on the bits with glue sticks.

Notes

For parents to pray with your child

Jesus, you were born as
a baby (rock baby in arms).
You worked as a carpenter,
sawing the wood.
(saw wood).
You died on a cross and
you rose again.
(arms out, then jump and
clap hands).
You are loving and kind
and good.
(put up fingers, counting
to three).
In heaven and on earth
your glory shines.
(point up and down then
trace big circle with fingers
stretched out).
You are loving and kind
and good.
(count on fingers again).

PENTECOST

Thought for the day

With great power the Spirit of God is poured out on the expectant disciples.

Readings

Acts 2:1-11
Psalm 103:1, 24, 29-31
1 Corinthians 12:3-7, 12-13
John 20:19-23

Aim

To celebrate the birthday of the Church.

Starter

Play with balloons, enjoying the way they float about in the air.

Teaching

Bring in a birthday cake with two candles on, each candle standing for a thousand years. Explain that today is the Church's birthday. 'Church' doesn't really mean the building, but the people inside. It means a group of Christians who are filled with God's love. That first happened at Pentecost, nearly two thousand years ago, when God's Holy Spirit was poured into the followers of Jesus, until they were filled with his love. So that's how old the Church is – nearly two thousand years old! Sing 'Happy birthday to you' to 'dear Church', and while the cake is being cut up, try the finger rhyme which reminds us that the Church is really the people inside, filled with God's love. (And all of us here are part of that Church.)

Here's the church,

here's the steeple,

open the doors

and here's all the people

Praying

We are the Church
and you are our God.
You fill us with love every day.
We are the Church
and you are our God.
We're a body of people who pray.

Activities

Today's sheet can be decorated and made into a Pentecost birthday hat, which the children can wear into church. They can also have another game, dancing and jumping about to some recorded praise songs. Every time the music stops, call out a name, and everyone prays for that person in the group. (Thank you, God, for Jessica. Fill her with your love.) Make sure every person is prayed for.

Notes

A   Join to B   B

cut here

cut here

We are the Church and you are our God.
You fill us with love every day.
We are the Church and you are our God.
We're a body of people who pray.

For parents to pray
with your child

FEASTS OF THE LORD

TRINITY SUNDAY

Thought for the day

The mystery of God – Creator, Redeemer and Sanctifier all at once – is beyond our human understanding, yet closer to us than breathing.

Readings

Exodus 34:4-6, 8-9
Daniel 3:52-56
2 Corinthians 13:11-13
John 3:16-18

Aim

To know that God is the greatest.

Starter

Play with sand and buckets, spades and pots, or with water, filling and emptying, and discovering that big amounts won't fit in small containers.

Teaching

Use examples from the starter activity to show how we can't fit big amounts into small containers. Our God is much greater and more wonderful than we can imagine, so it's not surprising that all he is won't fit into our little human minds!

But even though we cannot ever understand all that God is, we can certainly be best friends with him, and snuggle up in his loving, and know that he loves us and cares for us. It's all a bit like this.

There was once a puppy called Pete. He was very soft to stroke, very wriggly and he ran about a lot, and liked eating. Best of all he liked eating rabbit-flavoured crunchy biscuits, but he wasn't allowed many of those in case he got fat. Pete belonged to Oliver, who thought he was the best puppy in the world. Pete thought Oliver was the best boy in the world. They loved each other. Sometimes they played with a ball. Oliver threw the ball and Pete went racing after it, with his ears flying out behind him. He could catch the ball while it was still in the air! Then he would hang on to the ball so Oliver couldn't get it back, wagging his tail because it was such fun. But if Oliver started to walk away, Pete came racing over and dropped the ball at his feet, waiting for Oliver to throw it again.

Every day Oliver disappeared for a while. He didn't really disappear, of course; he just went to nursery school for the morning. Pete was puzzled and sad whenever Oliver disappeared, and he was happy and waggy as soon as Oliver came back. Because he was a dog, Pete couldn't understand things like people going to nursery school, and, however long Pete lives, he will never be able to understand things like that, any more than we will ever be able to understand everything about God.

But what Pete did know very well indeed was that he loved Oliver and Oliver loved him, and they both enjoyed being together. Whenever they played and laughed together, whenever Oliver fed him (especially rabbit-flavoured crunchy biscuits!) and whenever Pete fell asleep on Oliver's feet, he knew that he was loved and owned by someone very special, just as we know we are owned and loved by a wonderful God.

Praying

Our God is so BIG, so strong and so mighty,
there's nothing that he cannot do!
The rivers are his, the mountains are his,
the stars are his handiwork too!
Our God is so BIG, so strong and so mighty,
there's nothing that he cannot do!

Activities

On the sheet there is a pattern which the children can trace round and round to get a feel of how God is unending, and they can look at and colour the pictures to see the different aspects of God.

Notes

Corpus Christi

Thought for the day

Jesus Christ is the living bread; as we feed on him we share his life.

Readings

Deuteronomy 8:2-3, 14-16
Psalm 147
1 Corinthians 10:16-17
John 6:51-58

Activities

It is likely that Corpus Christi services for schools will not need a separate programme for children. However, I have included a worksheet for children in church today.

On the sheet there is a recipe in case the children want to try making bread at home. They can also colour the picture of Jesus sharing bread with his friends.

For parents to pray with your child

Dear Jesus,
I may not be able to see
you with my eyes but I
know you are here, loving
me and my family all the
time.
Thank you, Jesus.

Making bread

flour, dried yeast, pinch of salt

water

Here are some shapes

Bake bread in a hot oven for 15-20 minutes

ORDINARY TIME

SECOND SUNDAY OF THE YEAR

Thought for the day

Jesus is recognised and pointed out by John to be God's chosen one.

Readings

Isaiah 49:3, 5-6
Psalm 39:2, 4, 7-10
1 Corinthians 1:1-3
John 1:29-34

Aim

To know that we can tell others about Jesus.

Starter

Sit in a circle and play 'pass the smile'. You smile to the person next to you, and they smile to the next person until the smile has gone all round the circle. With very young children you can pass a big smiley face around the circle; with older ones you could also try a short message, such as 'God loves you! Pass it on', which they can whisper to each other.

Teaching

First tell a story about the way some good news is passed on from one person to the next. Use simple puppets (wooden spoons and spatulas with faces drawn on and paper clothes stuck on with blutack).

Justin was excited. That morning the postman had delivered an airmail letter from his Uncle Kent and Auntie Betty. They lived in California, in the USA, and Justin had never seen them. Every birthday they sent him a birthday card and an American present, and every Christmas they sent a Christmas card, an American Advent calendar, an American Christmas present, and a photograph of them and their family sitting smiling in front of their Christmas tree. They had a large black dog called Corby.

Although he had never seen them, Justin felt he knew and loved Uncle Kent and Auntie Betty already. He knew that Uncle Kent liked gardening and making bird tables out of wood. He knew that Auntie Betty made big chocolate cakes which you ate with ice cream. And he knew that they both loved getting the drawings and paintings he often

sent them, and that they kept a photo of Justin on the fridge in their kitchen.

In this airmail letter Uncle Kent and Auntie Betty said that they were able to come to England, and stay with Justin and his family. So that's why Justin and his mum and dad were so excited!

They would all be driving to the airport to meet them. 'How will I know who they are?' asked Justin. Dad got out the latest Christmas photo. 'We'll take this with us and that will help you recognise them,' he said.

When they got to the airport they stood at the barrier while lots of people walked towards them, pushing trolleys piled high with bags and cases. Justin kept looking at the photo and then at all the people. Suddenly he spotted them. Auntie Betty looked just like the sort of person who would bake chocolate cakes and serve them with ice cream. Uncle Kent looked just like the sort of person who would enjoy making wooden bird tables. And from their smiles as they saw Justin, he knew they were just the sort of people to like his drawings, and keep his photo on their fridge because their smiles told Justin that Uncle Kent and Auntie Betty really knew and loved him. 'Hi, you guys!' shouted Auntie Betty, and Uncle Kent wheeled their trolley towards them as fast as he could, with a big grin all over his face.

It was a lovely visit. Justin liked the way Auntie Betty and Uncle Kent spoke, and were interested in everything. He couldn't wait to have his best friend round to meet them. As soon as he could, he told Imogen about them.

'Auntie Betty and Uncle Kent are here from America,' said Justin.

'What are they like?' asked Imogen.

'Come round and see!' said Justin.

So Imogen came round to see, and by the end of the afternoon she, Justin and Auntie Betty had made a big chocolate cake, which they all ate – with ice cream.

'How about you help me make a wooden bird table tomorrow?' said Uncle Kent.

Justin and Imogen looked at one another. 'You bet!' they said.

Praying

Jesus, we haven't seen you
but we know you love us.
We want to get to know you
and enjoy your company. Amen.

Activities

On the sheet they can think about how Jesus shows that he loves them, and how they can tell their friends about Jesus.

THIRD SUNDAY OF THE YEAR

Thought for the day

The prophecies of Isaiah are fulfilled in a new and lasting way in Jesus of Nazareth.

Readings

Isaiah 8:23-9:3
Psalm 26:1, 4, 13-14
1 Corinthians 1:10-13, 17
Matthew 4:12-23

Aim

To know that God wants us all to be safe, free and happy.

Starter

Have a selection of toys which encourage co-operative play, such as a farm, train set and building blocks. Leaders and children play together, setting up a non-threatening environment for successful interaction and contentment.

Teaching

Use a few toys as 'puppets' to act out a situation in which one is not letting the others play happily. This toy's behaviour is stopping the others from being free. First time through ask the children to spot what is happening and offer solutions to the problem. Listen carefully to all the ideas, even the extremely impractical and decidedly unchristian ones! Help them to see it as a problem to solve, rather than as a downer on a particular person. Now have an action replay, and this time have one of the other toys explain to the one behaving badly that they can't play their game if the buildings keep getting knocked over or taken away. The toy listens and says s/he would like to play as well. They let him/her have some bricks to knock down, so everyone is set free to play as they like to.

All of us sometimes make life difficult for other people. Perhaps we feel grumpy so we start being nasty to someone else. Perhaps we want something someone else has so we take it away from them. We are all learning how to live in the loving way that Jesus shows us. God sets us free so we can set one another free.

Praying

Lord Jesus,
thank you for setting us free.
Help us to let others be free as well. Amen.

Activities

Using the sheet the children can make a moving picture to reinforce today's teaching. They will each need some card and string. Vary the amount of preparation already done by leaders according to the age and skills of each child in the group.

Notes

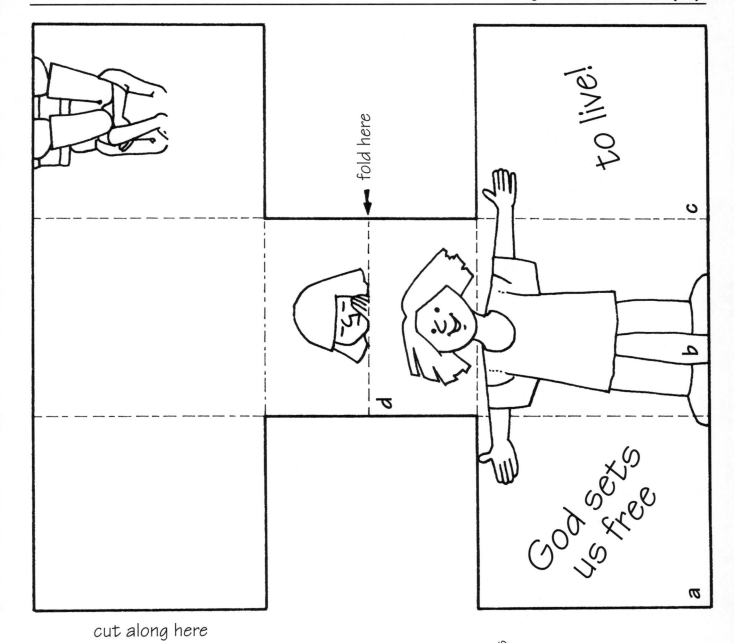

God sets us free

to live!

a

b

c

d

fold here

cut along here

For parents to pray
with your child

Lord Jesus,
thank you for
setting us free.
Help us to let others
be free as well.
Amen.

Colour the pop-up card
Cut out and fold at the middle
Stick the front and back together
Fold up like this:

1. **a** over **b**
2. **c** over **a**
3. **d** over **c**

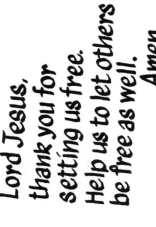

Open the card up to see what Jesus does

I am happy when I am . . .

Fourth Sunday
of the Year

Thought for the day

Happy are the poor in spirit, who are aware of their need of God.

Readings

Zephaniah 2:3; 3:12-13
Psalm 145
1 Corinthians 1:26-31
Matthew 5:1-12

Aim

To know that we are dependent on God for everything.

Starter

Have hidden around the room some different fruits, and a fruit bowl. Play some music, during which the children dance and jump about. When the music stops you call out, 'Fruit bowl!' and they find it and bring it to you. Then whenever the music stops a different fruit is called and has to be found and brought, until everything is found and the fruit bowl is full.

Teaching

Thank them all for their help in gathering the fruit, and enjoy looking together at the shape and colour of them. Everyone can say what their favourite fruit is. (Pass an orange round the circle so that only the person holding the orange is allowed to speak.)

All these good things to eat come from things God has made – including the fire to cook them. God has made us a lovely place to live on (it's planet earth) and he has made it so that there is good food to eat and people to play with and look after us. God gives us life, and all we need in life.

Praying

Thank you for the big round earth,
 (trace big circle in air with both hands)
thank you for the sky,
 (look up)
thank you for our food and drink,
 (pretend to eat and drink)
and trees that grow so high.
 (squat down, arm out to show tiny plant, and gradually stand up on to tiptoes, reaching arm up)
Your love is all around me,
 (turn around with arms out)
in front and behind.
 (point in front and behind)
I trust in you, my Father,
 (grip one hand with the other)
you are wonderfully kind!
 (arms up)

Activities

Have lots of pictures of God's provision (such as landscapes, fruit, flowers, animals and people) from magazines, calendars and greetings cards, and some sheets of coloured paper, so the children can choose pictures to stick on and make a group scrapbook to say 'Thank you' to God. There is space on the sheet for them to stick a picture or two, and a big 'Thank you' to colour in.

Notes

Thank you!

For parents to pray with your child

Thank you for the big round earth,
thank you for the sky,
thank you for our food and drink,
and trees that grow so high.
Your love is all around me,
in front and behind.
I trust in you, my Father,
you are wonderfully kind !

Fifth Sunday of the Year

Thought for the day

We are commissioned to live so that we shine like lights which direct others on to God, the source of Light.

Readings

Isaiah 58:7-10
Psalm 111:4-9
1 Corinthians 2:1-5
Matthew 5:13-16

Aim

To know what salt does and think about being like it.

Starter

A little makes a difference. Have a very quiet bell and give this to one of the children. Explain that whenever Suzie rings the bell, everyone freezes. Then get everyone moving and dancing around. Let each of the children have a turn at ringing the bell. It's only a little sound but look at what a difference it makes when it is used!

Teaching

Sit everyone in a circle and have a plate of plain crisps and a salt cellar in the middle of the circle. Explain that sometimes even little things can make a big difference – like our little bell in the game. Salt is like that. Spill a few grains (no more!) into everyone's hand to look at. The bits of salt aren't very big and we can't smell them, but we can certainly taste them. (If they want to, they can taste the salt in their hand.) What does the taste remind them of? We only need a little salt to flavour and bring out the taste of our food. For instance, a little salt on plain crisps helps us taste the nice potato flavour. They can all eat a crisp to notice this. Enjoy the eating of these together.

What would happen if we covered our food with salt? It would be bad for us, and we wouldn't taste anything except salt! So the job of salt is to bring out the good taste of other things.

Guess what Jesus said once – he said God wants us as his friends to be like salt! This is what he meant. Even if there aren't many of us, and even if we aren't very big, we can still make a big difference to the world, and help it to be a kinder, fairer and more loving place. The little bits of salt on the crisps help us to taste the real potato, and God wants us to be so loving and friendly to people that they feel happy and free. Instead of going around making people frightened, or making life hard work for them, God wants us to help people, and let them know we care about them.

Praying

Dear Jesus,
I would like to be like salt
and help people
to enjoy being themselves. Amen.

Activities

On the activity sheet there are some little things to search for, and some pictures of Jesus' friends being salt. There is also a label to colour which they can stick on to their salt mill at home.

Notes

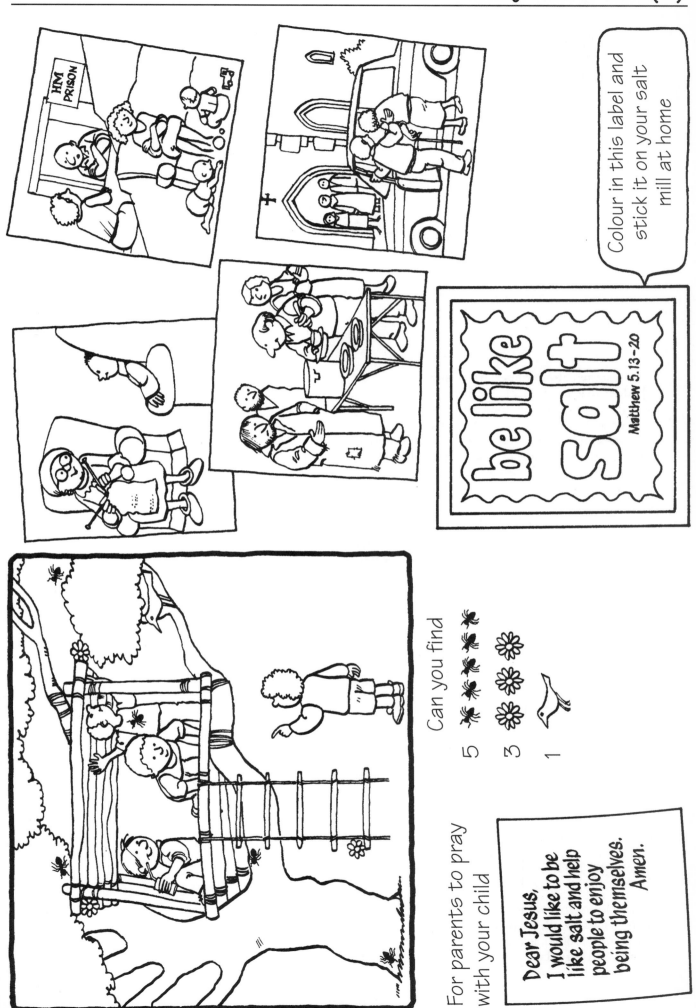

SIXTH SUNDAY OF THE YEAR

Thought for the day

To live God's way is to choose the way of life.

Readings

Ecclesiasticus 15:15-20
Psalm 118:1-2, 4-5, 17-18, 33-34
1 Corinthians 2:6-10
Matthew 5:17-37

Aim

To know that God's way is the way of love.

Starter

Using some cut-out paper arrow signs, two of the children go with a leader to lay a trail. The others then go off in pairs to follow the trail, so that eventually everyone should end up at the same place. Make sure the children are supervised very carefully, and that the trail is within sight of a leader all the time. (Or use the Gold Panners group to work with the Treasure Seekers on this.)

Teaching

We followed the way Zac and Phoebe led us because we followed the arrows they left. Today we are going to find out what God's way is, so that we can follow that in our lives.

Ask them to follow these instructions:

- Walk quickly
- Creep quietly
- Clap loudly
- Sit silently
- Smile happily
- Frown crossly

Praise everyone for following the instructions so well. Jesus tells us that to follow him we are to live lovingly. All get up and hold hands in a circle as you talk about ways to live lovingly when we are at home/at playgroup/visiting grandparents and so on. Talk about how to live lovingly with different people (such as people who are sad/have got a headache/want to play with your toys.) Then walk round, still holding hands, singing these words to the tune of *Frère Jacques*.

Follow Jesus, follow Jesus
walk his way, walk his way,
loving one another, loving one another
every day, every day.

Praying

Lead on, Jesus, I will follow!
I want to live your way,
loving you and loving other people. Amen.

Activities

On the activity sheet there are other trails to follow, and a signpost to make which helps them remember that Jesus' way is the way of love. They will each need a short stick (about 6 centimetres long) and some glue.

Notes

SEVENTH SUNDAY OF THE YEAR

Thought for the day

We are called to be holy; to be perfect in our generous loving, because that is what God our Father is like.

Readings

Leviticus 19:1-2, 17-18
Psalm 102:1-4, 8, 10, 12-13
1 Corinthians 3:16-23
Matthew 5:38-48

Aim

To know that God wants us to love one another as he loves us.

Starter

Bring along lots of cartons and boxes and place them all over the room. Tell the children we are going to build a high tower, and let them help by collecting boxes and bringing them over to add to the tower.

Teaching

Show the children the comedy trick of having your own hands behind your back while your partner's arms pretend to be yours. Try talking and gesticulating, and try to eat or drink something! Enjoy the silliness of it, and then get everyone to look at the way we train our own arms to look after all our needs. Suppose your nose itches – what happens? One of your arms stretches out to exactly the right itchy place and scratches it better for you. Suppose you want to eat a biscuit? One of your arms gets hold of the biscuit and holds it for you, bringing it up to your mouth every time you want to take a bite.

It isn't just our arms we use. If we want to get across the room to see out of the window, we get our legs to take us over there. We don't have to wait for them while they finish what they are doing, or just sit and watch a bit more television. They do what we want straightaway. That's because we love ourselves, and do our best to make sure we are comfortable.

God's idea for us is that we should love one another like that. That means noticing what other people are needing and going to help them. Let's try it.

Suppose Mum is trying to carry lots of bags out of the supermarket. (Act this out with real bags from the local store.) Get the children to suggest ways they could do some practical loving. Suppose it's time for the cat to be fed and her bowl is empty. (Have a bowl and some dry cat food.) The children can suggest how to do the loving. Suppose Dad is feeling very fed up because his team has lost an important match. (Mime this.) How can they do the loving?

Teach the children this 'love your neighbour as yourself' code to help them remember:

- Look (make hands into binoculars and look around)
- Think (put finger to head thoughtfully)
- Do (stretch out hands)

Praying

The more love we give,
the more love there is!
Help us to spread your love around
so there's lots and lots and lots! Amen.

Activities

On the sheet there is a picture to which the children can add lots of apples, lots of flowers and lots of sunshine and raindrops. There is also a picture to spot the loving going on, and the needs which are not being noticed by the people in the drawing.

Notes

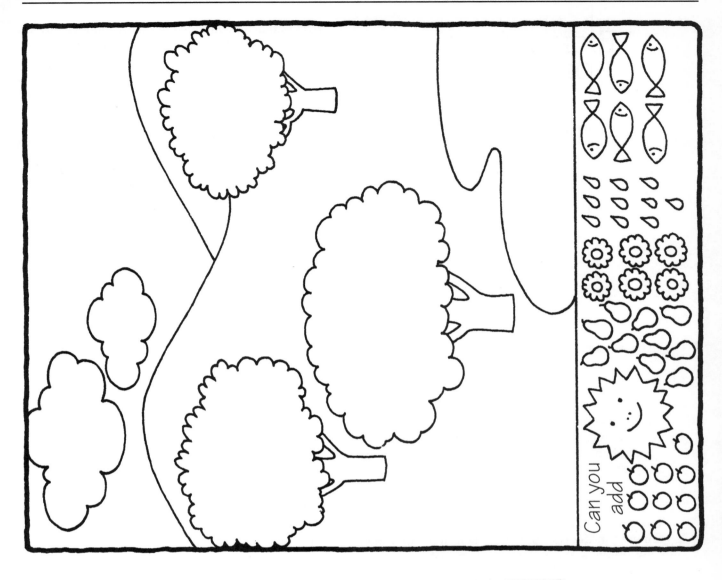

Can you add

Spot the loving, spot the needs!

For parents to pray with your child

The more love we give, the more love there is! Help us to spread your love around so there's lots and lots and lots! Amen.

EIGHTH SUNDAY OF THE YEAR

Thought for the day

God is creative and good; seeking his rule, as our priority, will mean that everything else falls into place.

Readings

Isaiah 49:14-15
Psalm 61:2-3, 6-9
1 Corinthians 4:1-5
Matthew 6:24-34

Aim

To know that God made the world and looks after us.

Starter

Using either a real baby and parent or a baby doll, have someone talking about looking after a new baby, bathing and feeding, and showing some of the normal baby equipment like rattles and shampoo, nappies and bibs.

Teaching

Talk over the loving care parents give their babies, bringing in the way they may help look after any baby brothers and sisters. Explain that God loves and looks after us like that, noticing what we need, comforting us when we are sad, and sorting us out when we get into a mess. Just as we can help our parents in the care of our brothers and sisters, so we can work with God in helping to look after one another, because we are all brothers and sisters in God's family.

Look at some pictures of God's world to see what a beautiful place God has given us to live in. We can help look after the world as well as the people who live in it.

Praying

Thank you, God,
for making us such a lovely world to live in.
Help us to look after it
and the other people who live here. Amen.

Activities

Using a paper plate each and some salt dough (two cups of flour, one cup of salt, and water to mix) the children can make a model animal and put it in a suitable landscape, following the instructions below. There is also a dot-to-dot puzzle on the worksheet.

Add to the dots provided or delete some according to the age and ability of the children in your group.

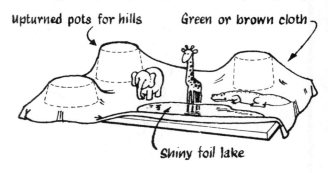

Upturned pots for hills   Green or brown cloth

Shiny foil lake

Notes

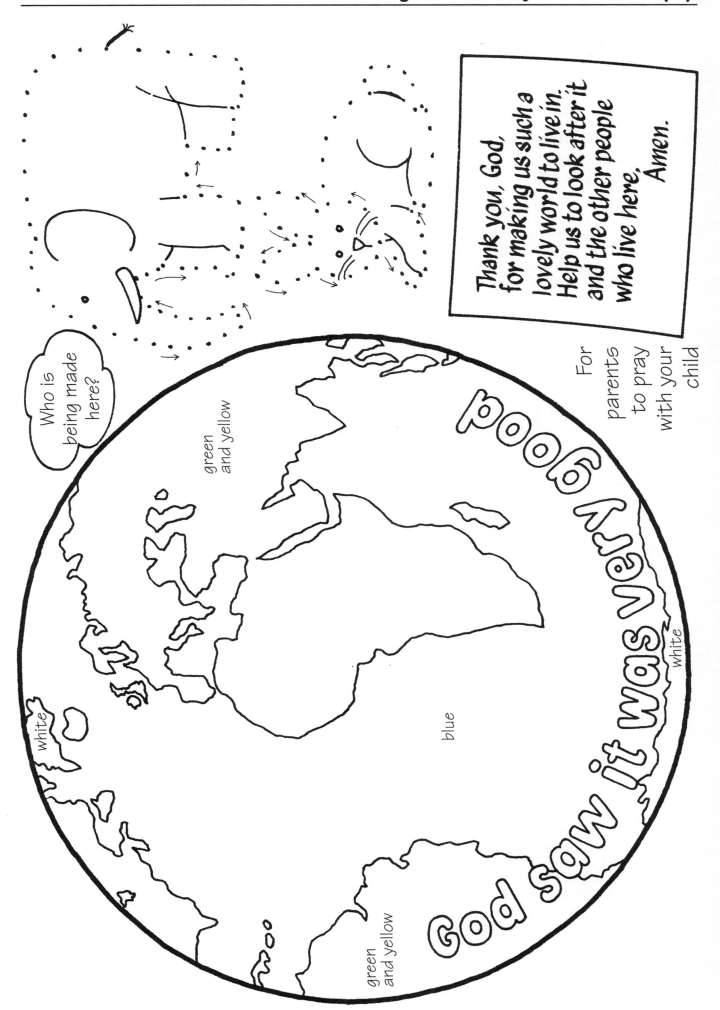

NINTH SUNDAY OF THE YEAR

Thought for the day

Wise listeners build their lives up on the strong rock of the word of God.

Readings

Deuteronomy 11:18, 26-28
Psalm 30:2-4, 17, 25
Romans 3:21-25, 28
Matthew 7:21-27

Aim

To know that Jesus is like strong rock to build on.

Starter

Bring along plenty of construction toys, such as Duplo, blocks or simply lots of boxes and cartons, and work with the children to build.

Teaching

Jesus was once talking to his friends and he told them this: 'All the things I teach you to do are very important, and will help you live a good life. Wise people will listen to what I teach them (*cup hand to ear as you say this*) and then do it (*open hands up*). Foolish people will hear what I tell them (*cup hand to ear*) and yet do nothing about it (*fold arms*).'

Explain that you are going to tell them all something, and they can choose whether to listen (*cup hand to ear*) and then do what you say (*open hands*) or just listen (*cup hand to ear*) and do nothing about it (*fold arms*). Tell them that you have some sweets in a tin. Only children who put their hands up will be given one. They can now choose whether to put their hands up or not. Then give out sweets to those with their hands up.

It is wise and sensible to do what Jesus tells us, because he loves us and knows what is best for us all. But lots of people are not very wise. They hear what Jesus says, and yet do nothing about it. Jesus said, 'If you listen to what I tell you (*cup hand to ear*) and do what I have said (*open hands up*) you will be as sensible and wise as a person building on a good strong rock. If you listen to what I tell you (*cup hand to ear*) and yet do nothing about it (*fold arms*) you will be as silly and foolish as a person building on wobbly, moving sand!'

Let's see what happens if we build on rock (which is strong, like this floor). Build up on this and see how firm the house is. Let's see what happens if we build on wobbly, moving sand. Have a floppy surface such as an old pillow, or rumpled blanket and pretend that is sand, because it is wobbly and moves about a bit, like sand. Even if you carefully manage to keep your building together while you are building, as soon as the pillow or blanket is jogged the whole building collapses. (Do this as you speak.)

So if we are going to build up good strong lives, let's not be foolish, listening to what Jesus says (*cup hands to ears*) and doing nothing about it (*fold arms*). Let's make sure we are wise, listening to what Jesus tells us (*cup hands to ears*) and doing what he says (*open hands*).

Praying

Jesus, I don't want to be foolish,
hearing what you tell me
    (*cup hand to ear*)
but not doing anything about it.
    (*fold arms*)
Jesus, I want to be wise,
hearing what you tell me
    (*cup hand to ear*)
and doing it in my life.
    (*open hands*)

Activities

Each child will need a strip of thin card so they can stick their house models on to it and stand them up. Also on the sheet, a picture with some people doing what Jesus said, and some not, helps them notice the godly way of living and the contrasting selfish way.

Notes

For parents to pray with your child

Jesus, I don't want to be foolish
hearing what you tell me (cup hand to ear)
but not doing anything about it (fold arms)
Jesus I want to be wise, hearing what
you tell me (cup hand to ear)
and doing it in my life (open hands)

Who's living God's way?

Build wisely

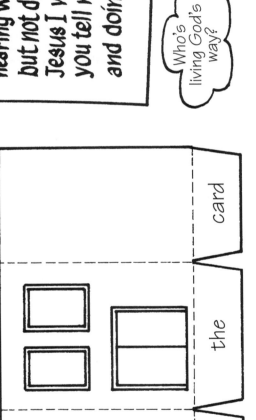

Stick   on to   the   card

Colour your house and cut it out
Stick it on a card base
Decorate the garden and stick
on the prayer
Make a tree and stick
it on

TENTH SUNDAY OF THE YEAR

Thought for the day

Jesus' life of healing and compassion acts out God's desire for mercy rather than empty sacrifice.

Readings

Hosea 6:3-6
Psalm 49:1, 8, 12-15
Romans 4:18-25
Matthew 9:9-13

Aim

To know that Jesus made people better.

Starter

Sit in a circle and pass round a teddy with bandage on him. Each person holding the teddy can share with the others about a time they were poorly, or what it is like to be poorly.

Teaching

Hold up a picture (from a children's Bible) of Jesus healing someone which is covered up by a piece of card. Explain that before Jesus came, people couldn't see what God was like. But when Jesus came to live on earth (uncover the picture) they could see that God was very kind, because Jesus was always very kind. What is he doing in this picture? He is making someone better. Jesus hated to see people suffering and being poorly, and often he would make them better. Today we are going to hear about a child who was very ill at the time Jesus was living on earth.

Unroll a bed mat (this can be a blanket) and explain that this is the kind of bed that people slept on in those days. The child was feeling very, very ill, and her mummy put her to bed. (Have one of the children to lie on the bed.) Just like you, when you are ill, her mummy and daddy probably stroked her face, wiped her hot head with nice, cool water, and gave her water to drink. (Do these things as you speak.) Her daddy and mummy were worried about their daughter, because instead of getting better, as usually happens, she got more and more ill.

Then they heard from a friend that Jesus was walking to their town. They had heard that Jesus was very kind, and that he could make people better, and they badly wanted their daughter better, because they loved her so much. But before Jesus got to the town, their daughter died, and everyone was very sad. 'Well,' said the girl's daddy, 'I'm still going to ask him to come!', and he got up and ran out of the house towards Jesus. 'Jesus!' he said, 'my daughter has just died! But if you come and touch her with your hand I'm sure she will live again!'

Jesus felt very sorry for this man and his family. He wanted to help them, and said that of course he would come. When they got to the house everyone was crying and making a lot of noise. Jesus told them to go away. 'The child is not dead,' he said. 'She is only asleep.' The people laughed at that, but they went out and left Jesus with the little girl and her mummy and daddy. He went to where she was lying and held her hand. The little girl started to open her eyes! She looked at Jesus and smiled. She looked at her mummy and daddy and smiled. Then she got up from her bed mat. 'Thank you, Jesus!' she said. 'I feel better than I have for ages!' And they all hugged one another and cried again – but this time because they were so happy.

Praying

Jesus, you are kind; Jesus, you are loving.
You made people happy and you made people well.
Jesus, you are kind; Jesus, you are loving –
so God is kind and loving, I can tell.

Activities

On the sheet there is a picture of a child, ill in bed, and they can draw in the things that might make them feel better. They can also colour, cut out and put in the right order the pictures of today's story. Provide them with strips of coloured paper to stick the pictures on to, then fold the strip of paper to make a zigzag book.

Notes

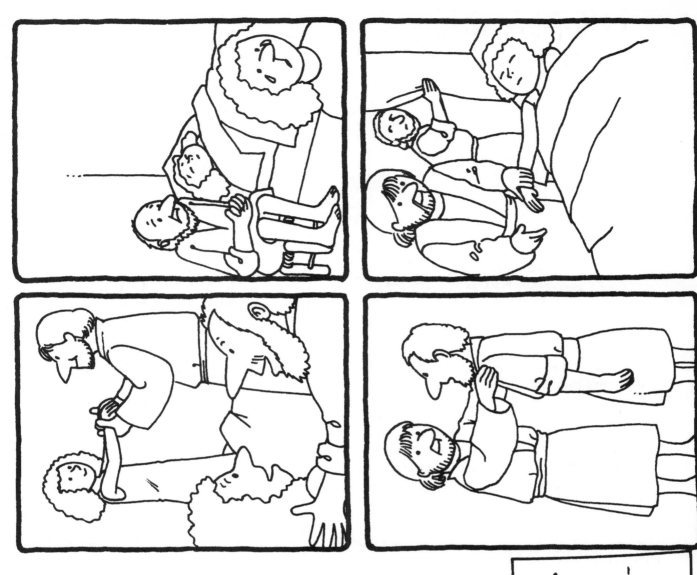

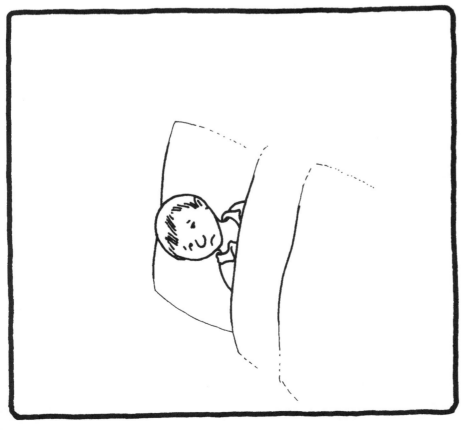

For parents to pray with your child

Jesus you are kind, Jesus you are loving.
You made people happy and you made
people well.
Jesus you are kind, Jesus you are loving–
So God is kind and loving, I can tell.

ELEVENTH SUNDAY OF THE YEAR

Thought for the day

Jesus sends his ambassadors out to proclaim God's kingdom and bring hope and peace of mind to the harassed and lost in every age.

Readings

Exodus 19:2-6
Psalm 99:2-3, 5
Romans 5:6-11
Matthew 9:36-10:8

Aim

To know that Jesus chose twelve followers to teach, and to work with him.

Starter

As the children arrive, give them a piece of paper with their name written on it, which they can decorate. Then they all hold their names as they jump about to some music. When the music stops choose a name, and that child comes to stick their label on a poster titled 'We are the Treasure Seekers'. Continue until everyone has been chosen, and the names are all stuck on the poster.

Teaching

Count to twelve with various things – leaves, stones, toys and crayons, for example. Then try counting to twelve together, using fingers of both hands and stamping each foot.

When Jesus was living on our earth he often taught crowds and crowds of people. They would all come out in the sunshine to the beach or the hills, and sit down to listen to what Jesus said. There were mums and dads, babies, toddlers, teenagers, uncles and aunties, grandmas and grandads. Jesus enjoyed teaching all the people and showing them God's love.

He didn't just talk to the crowds. He also chose some people to be his followers, so he could spend time with them and train them ready for when he had gone back to heaven. Can you guess how many people he chose? It was one, two, three, four, five, six, seven, eight, nine, ten, eleven, twelve! As you all count, place on the floor twelve paper shapes of people, based on the pictures below. They were all in Jesus' gang – they were like a class

and Jesus was their teacher. As they walked along or sat around the fire in the evening eating their supper, Jesus would talk to them, and answer their questions. They were called *disciples*.

One day Jesus sent his one, two, three, four, five, six, seven, eight, nine, ten, eleven, twelve disciples out to try teaching the people in all the towns and villages round about, and making people better. They would be doing the kind of work Jesus usually did. Did he send them out with posh shoes? (Put a pair down.) No! Did he send them out with lots of spare clothes in a bag? (Put a bag down.) No! Did he send them out with lots of money to spend? (Put down a purse and cheque book.) No! He sent them out just as they were, with his blessing, and his prayers and his love.

Praying

Jesus chose
1 2 3 4 5 6 7 8 9 10 11 12 disciples
and told them all about God's love.
They told others, who told others, who told others
who told ME! So I know, too!
Thank you, Jesus.

Activities

If you have a set of Russian dolls, bring these along to show the children how the news gets passed on from person to person. Use a person shape cut from polystyrene so that the children can print twelve disciples in their places on the sheet. Make sure you protect clothing during the painting process.

For parents to pray with your child

Jesus chose
1 2 3 4 5 6 7 8 9 10 11 12
disciples
and told them all about God's love
They told others, who told others,
who told others
who told ME!
So I know too!
Thank you, Jesus.

Twelfth Sunday of the Year

Thought for the day

When we are willing to take up our cross with Jesus we will also know his risen life.

Readings

Jeremiah 20:10-13
Psalm 68:8-10, 14, 17, 33-35
Romans 5:12-15
Matthew 10:26-33

Aim

To know that we can use our bodies for good.

Starter

Draw some signs on separate pieces of card: eyes, ears, hands, mouth, feet and a whole body outline. When the whole body sign is shown, everyone dances around to some music. Whenever the music stops, one of the other signs is shown and everyone holds that bit of their body until the music starts again.

Teaching

Tell the children how God has made us with these lovely bodies that can do all sorts of things. Place the signs from the starter activity on the floor, face down, and uncover them one by one, as you talk together about all the things these parts of us can do. They can demonstrate some of them, too. Focus on all the positives, so that you are celebrating the way we can work in God's team for good.

Praying

Thank you, God, for this body of mine.
It can shout and help and play.
I like to use this body of mine
to show your love each day. Amen.

Activities

On the sheet there is a picture of a person to which the children can add various parts by drawing them, or you could cut out the appropriate parts beforehand and the children can stick them on.

Notes

Draw or stick on the missing bits!

Draw yourself doing the loving you are thinking about

For parents to pray with your child

Thank you, God, for this body of mine.
It can shout and help and play.
I like to use this body of mine
to show your love each day.
Amen.

Thirteenth Sunday of the Year

Thought for the day

As Christ's people we are no longer slaves to sin, but available for righteousness.

Readings

2 Kings 4:8-11, 14-16
Psalm 88:2-3, 16-19
Romans 6:3-4, 8-11
Matthew 10:37-42

Aim

To be introduced to the idea of taking up something hard, and sometimes painful, out of love.

Starter

Play the singing game 'The princess slept for one hundred years', which includes the handsome prince cutting the forest with his sword in order to reach the beautiful princess.

Teaching

Tell the children this story, either reading it to them or preferably memorising the main points and telling it with your own character.

In Africa there was a village, and in the village there lived a girl called Eunice and her three brothers and her mother. Her father had to work in a big town a long way off, so he was not often at home. Every day Eunice and her little brothers went out with their mother, and all the other mothers, to fetch the water, because in their village there were no taps to get their water from. They walked quite a long way out of the village, until they came to a place where the water bubbled up out of the ground. The children played in the water while the mothers lifted down their heavy pots from their heads and filled them with water. Then the water pots were lifted high on to the heads of all the mothers, who were very strong, and everyone walked (more slowly, this time) back to the village, with enough water for the day.

One morning Eunice woke up to find that her mother was very ill. She was hot and shivery, and could not get up. One of the older women in the village came in to sit with her, but the family still needed the water to be fetched. Who could do that? Eunice thought to herself, 'I will get the water today for my mother.'

So she went down with her brothers and the other mothers, carrying the bucket, and when they got to the place where the water bubbled up out of the ground, she filled the bucket up to the brim. It was very heavy to carry, but Eunice kept thinking of her mother at home, and how happy she would be to have the water collected for the day, and somehow that made it easier to keep going. Some of Eunice's friends were playing together and they called out to her, 'Hey, Eunice, put that bucket down and come and play with us!' Eunice loved playing with her friends, but she knew that today it was more important to get the water home to give her mother a drink, and save her worrying. So she called back, 'Not today, I can't. I have the water to carry home.'

It seemed a very long walk back to the village, but at last Eunice reached the house, and carried the water inside. Her mother was lying there, weak and ill, but when she looked up and saw Eunice with the bucket full of water for the day, she smiled, and whispered, 'Well done, my child. God bless you for your kind heart!' Eunice ran and gave her a drink, and wiped her mother's head with some cool water. Suddenly it didn't matter that the bucket had been so heavy to carry, or that her muscles ached. She had carried it out of love.

Praying

Dear Jesus,
you gave up everything for us
because you love us.
Help us to do loving things
for one another
even if they are hard work. Amen.

Activities

On the sheet there is a week's chart for them to fill in when they do something kind for someone else, and there are some pictures of ideas to help them. It would also be nice for the group to do something kind and thoughtful, such as gathering up the litter outside (or inside!) or preparing a song to sing for the rest of the congregation in church.

Notes

Sunday   Monday   Tuesday   Wednesday   Thursday   Friday   Saturday

It's good to be kind! See me being kind this week!

For parents to pray with your child

Dear Jesus,
you gave up everything for us because you love us.
Help us to do loving things for one another even if they are hard work. Amen.

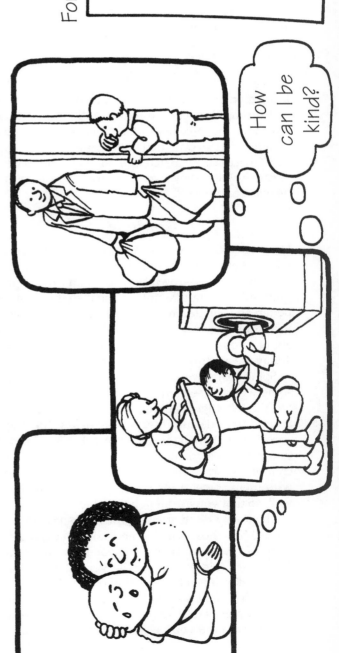

How can I be kind?

FOURTEENTH SUNDAY OF THE YEAR

Thought for the day

To all who are weary with carrying heavy burdens in life, Jesus offers rest for our souls and unthreatening relief.

Readings

Zechariah 9:9-10
Psalm 144:1-2, 8-11, 13-14
Romans 8:9, 11-13
Matthew 11:25-30

Aim

To know that we can tell Jesus all that weighs us down, and he will help us.

Starter

Bring along five or six items which the children can pick up as they choose which is the lightest and which is the heaviest. Make this fairly obvious weight-wise, except that the shapes and weights don't necessarily match up, so they might get a surprise when they expect a large item to be the heaviest and it isn't.

Teaching

Have one of the leaders struggling in with several bulky, heavy parcels. You greet them and comment on how weighed-down they look, and they agree, gratefully letting you unload them so they can feel better and sit down comfortably. They ask what we're doing today, and the children can tell them about choosing the heaviest and lightest parcel. Today we are thinking about carrying heavy loads.

Some loads we can see (like these parcels) but some we can't see – like when we are feeling very worried about something, and we carry our worry around with us and it feels quite heavy. (Pick up a parcel and hold it as you speak.) What kind of things do we sometimes worry about a lot? Ask the children to share their ideas about this, and share with them some of the things you worry about as well, so that you are all in it together.

The lovely thing about knowing Jesus is that we can tell him those worries, and ask him to help sort them out with us. (Have someone take the parcel from you.) And just talking it over with our friend Jesus makes it feel less worrying.

Another load we can't see is being frightened about something. (Pick up another load.) We carry that fear around with us and it can make us scared and sad. What kind of things are we scared and frightened about? Once again, share these together. Well, what's good about knowing Jesus is that we can tell him our fears, and ask him to help us be brave. (Have this load taken from you.) Jesus is never too busy to listen to us, and we can talk to him any time and anywhere. He will always be there for us because he loves us, and doesn't want us struggling along with heavy loads all the time – he wants us to be free to skip and run and play!

Praying

Heavy loads, heavy loads,
    (pretend to carry them)
'I'm worried!' and 'I'm scared!'
    (head in hands, then shake with fright)
'Come to me,' says Jesus,
    (beckon)
'and I will give you rest!'
    (arms out, palms up)
Thank you, thank you, Jesus!
    (jump up and down and clap hands)
You really are the best!
    (both hands up in air)

Activities

Give each child a stone to decorate with paint or stickers which they can put on the mat which they make from the sheet. Then they can use their 'worry stone' to remind them to talk things over each day with their friend Jesus.

Notes

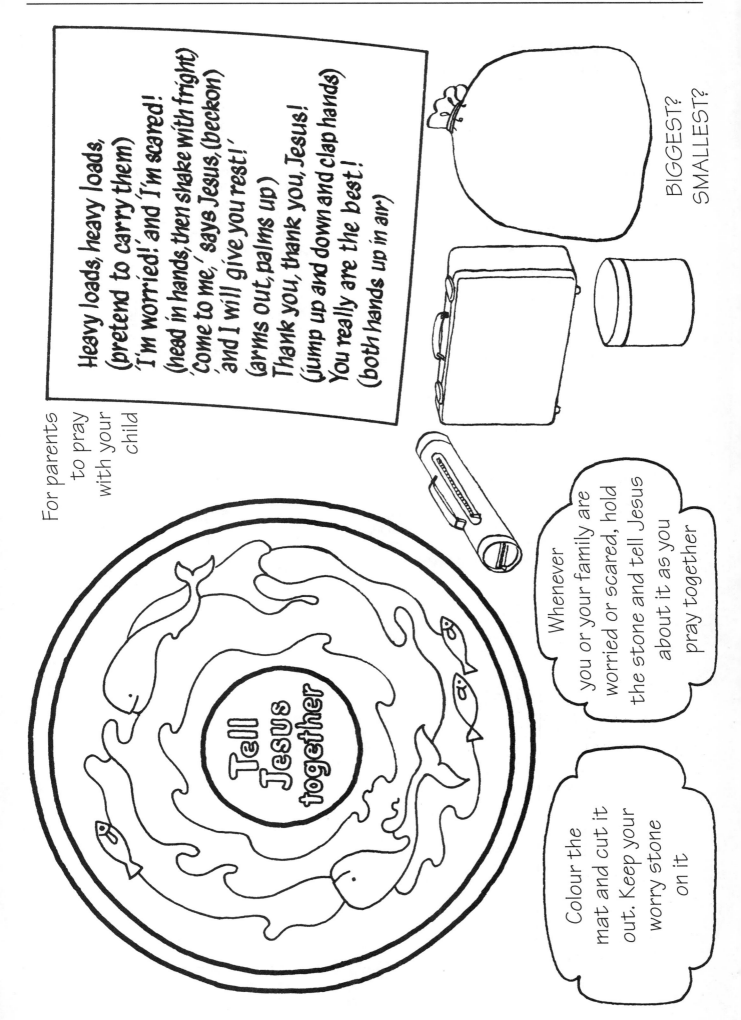

For parents to pray with your child

Heavy loads, heavy loads,
(pretend to carry them)
'I'm worried! and I'm scared!
(head in hands, then shake with fright)
'Come to me,' says Jesus, (beckon)
'and I will give you rest!'
(arms out, palms up)
Thank you, thank you, Jesus!
(jump up and down and clap hands)
You really are the best!
(both hands up in air)

BIGGEST? SMALLEST?

Tell Jesus together

Whenever you or your family are worried or scared, hold the stone and tell Jesus about it as you pray together

Colour the mat and cut it out. Keep your worry stone on it

Fifteenth Sunday of the Year

Thought for the day

Seed of God's word, sown in good soil, watered by his rain and warmed by his sunlight, produces a good crop of spiritual fruit.

Readings

Isaiah 55:10-11
Psalm 64:10-14
Romans 8:18-23
Matthew 13:1-23

Aim

To know that God sends the rain to water the land and make things grow.

Starter

A rainy game. You will need either two tape recorders, so that you can play 'sunny' music from one and 'rainy' music from the other, or two different types of sounds, such as a rainstick and a xylophone. One of the leaders holds a large golfing umbrella. Play the sunny and the rainy music or sounds to the children. Whenever they hear the sunny sound, they skip about in the sunshine, and whenever they hear the rainy sound, they run to take shelter under the umbrella.

Teaching

Start with this puzzle song about water, the children joining in with the chorus. (See page 144 for the music.)

1. You can drink it, swim in it,
   cook and wash up in it,
   fish can breathe in it –
   what can it be?

   It's water!
   God has provided us water!
   Water of life.

2. It's as hard as rock,
   yet it flows down a mountain,
   and clouds drop drips of it –
   what can it be?

3. It's as light as snowflakes
   and heavy as hailstones,
   as small as dewdrops
   and big as the sea.

Show the children a large cut-out cloud, and talk with them about what it feels like to be out in the rain, and what they wear in the rain. What happens to the ground when it rains? Talk about puddles and sloppy mud. What happens to the plants and flowers when it rains? Show the children a daisy or buttercup, still attached to its root, and tell them how the plant drinks up the water through the roots, and that helps it to grow. After a long time without rain the grass looks all dry and brown, but after rain everywhere is lovely and green again.

God sends the rain so that everything can live and grow. We all need the rain – we couldn't live without it! Rain is one of the many ways God showers us with good gifts.

Praying

This is a water cycle prayer as it goes round and round!

Thank you, God, for sending rain,
pitter, patter, pitter, patter,
it makes the grass all green again,
pitter, patter, pitter, patter,
it makes the fruit and veggies grow,
pitter, patter, pitter, patter,
we all need water to live, and so . . .
pitter, patter, pitter, patter,
thank you, God, for sending rain!

Activities

Using the picture on the sheet the children can make a water cycle wheel. They will need to stick it on to thin card and poke a stick or pencil through the middle as shown. They can also have shiny paper raindrop shapes to tie on to string, which they can shake about as they come into church as a refreshing shower of rain. (Arrange this with whoever is leading the worship in church.)

Notes

Spot 2 umbrellas the same. How many altogether?

For parents to pray with your child
(This is a water cycle prayer as it goes round and round)

Thank you, God, for sending rain,
pitter, patter, pitter, patter,
it makes the grass all green again,
pitter, patter, pitter, patter,
it makes the fruit and veggies grow,
pitter, patter, pitter, patter,
we all need water to live,
and so...
pitter, patter, pitter, patter,
thank you, God, for sending rain!

Sixteenth Sunday of the Year

Thought for the day

God's justice is always blended with mercy and loving kindness, so that we have real hope.

Readings

Wisdom of Solomon 12:13, 16-19
Psalm 85:5-6, 9-10, 15-16
Romans 8:26-27
Matthew 13:24-43

Aim

To know that God is fair and kind.

Starter

Split an apple or a bar of chocolate up among everyone so that it is exactly fair, and everyone gets a piece if they want it. In a time of news-sharing, go round the circle in order, so that no one is left out and all are asked if they would like to share some of their news. Don't let anyone get an extra go just because they are noisy or attention-seeking.

Teaching

You will need four puppets, or you can make your own from old socks or wooden spoons. You don't need four hands, though – just pick up the one which is talking at any one time. One puppet is baby-sitting, and trying to give out biscuits fairly, but two of the 'children' are so demanding and noisy that they end up getting more than the other. The third child complains that it isn't fair. Why should they get more just because they're noisy?

Stop the puppets and ask the children what they think should happen. Then have a nearly-action-replay with the baby-sitter telling the noisy ones that the biscuits will be shared out fairly, which means one each, and being noisy won't make any difference.

Now have the puppets being a parent and children buying an ice-cream each. The parent tells the children to be very careful not to drop them. One child does drop the ice-cream, and cries about it. The parent is sympathetic, and says, 'You can share mine!'

God is like a loving mum or dad who is always fair, but very kind as well, and helps us out when we make mistakes.

Praying

Jesus, I'm glad you are always fair.
You love us all, and don't leave anyone out.
And when we make mistakes
you help us put things right again.

Activities

They can give everyone in the picture on the sheet the same things, so it is fair. This can either be done by drawing the items in, or you could provide separate, pre-cut items which they stick on.

Notes

a lollipop

Well done for being fair!

Give each child

a hat

a pet cat

Are there enough shoes for the feet?

For parents to pray with your child

Jesus, I'm glad you are always fair.
You love us all, and don't leave anyone out.
And when we make mistakes you help us put things right again.

SEVENTEENTH SUNDAY OF THE YEAR

Thought for the day

Jesus, the teacher, enables the ordinary, unlearned people to understand God's wisdom – the eternal laws of his Father's kingdom.

Readings

1 Kings 3:5, 7-12
Psalm 118:57, 72, 76-77, 127-130
Romans 8:28-30
Matthew 13:44-52

Aim

To know that finding Jesus is like finding treasure.

Starter

Have a treasure hunt where each child experiences the hunting and the discovering. To do this, wrap each 'treasure' in paper tied with a different coloured piece of wool. Give each child a matching piece of wool and send them off to find their own treasure.

Teaching

Talk about what fun it was to find the treasure. Today we are going to hear a story about finding treasure. It is one of the stories that Jesus told.

There was once a man who was digging in a field. He had been digging for most of the morning when his spade hit something hard. At first he thought it was a big stone. He dug around to find the edge of the stone so that he could lift it out. But this hard stone was straight at the edges and very flat at the top. 'What a funny stone!' thought the man, and he bent down and started to scrape away the earth to uncover it. 'This isn't a stone at all!' said the man to himself. 'It's more of a strong box. Whoever would want to bury a box in the middle of a field? How very strange.'

Very carefully he dug all round the edges of the box and brushed away earth until he could get his spade right underneath it. Slowly the box started to come out of the ground. It was heavy work and the man was using all his strength. 'Nearly there!' he kept saying to himself. 'We're nearly there!' Suddenly the last of the box popped out and the man fell over backwards and rolled over. 'Whoopsadaisy!' he said and crawled back on his hands and knees to see what he had dug up.

It was a strong wooden box with a clasp to hold it shut. The man opened it a tiny bit and peered inside. 'Slugs and earthworms, what have we here?' he gasped. Inside the box was a gleam of gold. It was full of shiny things and sparkling things. The man was so surprised that he slammed the box shut, and then, very slowly, he opened it again so that the sun shone down on all the treasure and the treasure shone and sparkled back at the sun. At first the man could hardly believe his eyes. But he blinked and the treasure was still there. He pinched himself and it hurt. 'Ouch! It must be real and this must be my lucky day!' shouted the man, and he did a little dance all by himself in the middle of the field.

'Now', thought the man, 'what I need to do is to buy this field, and then the treasure will be mine. But fields cost a lot of money, which I haven't got. Let's see . . . I could sell my table and chairs . . . and my old car . . . and my stamp collection . . . and . . . and . . .' The man worked very hard that afternoon. First he buried the box safely back in the field. Then he went home and got together everything he owned and had a car boot sale. He even sold the car boot – with the rest of the car thrown in for free! Then he went and bought the field.

Full of excitement, the man ran back to his field and started digging. It had been well worth getting rid of everything else. This time the box of sparkling treasure belonged to him, and he would be rich for the rest of his life!

Praying

Jesus, you are the treasure of my life!
With your love I am rich for ever and ever.

Activities

On the sheet there is a treasure chest for the children to fill with shiny, sparkling things. Have ready a selection of different coloured sparkling and shiny paper, and gold-sprayed pasta in different shapes, so that they can stick them into the chest.

Notes

Find another like this:

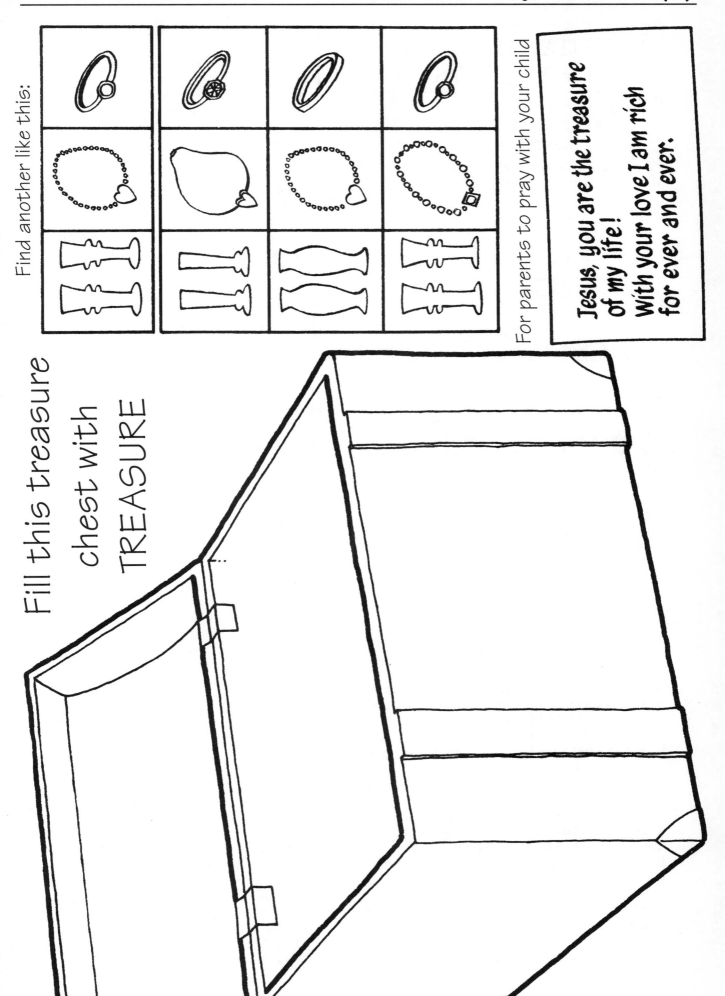

For parents to pray with your child

Jesus, you are the treasure of my life! With your love I am rich for ever and ever.

Fill this treasure chest with TREASURE

Eighteenth Sunday of the Year

Thought for the day

God feeds all who come to him hungry, and we, as the Church, are expected to share in that work.

Readings

Isaiah 55:1-3
Psalm 144:8-9, 15-18
Romans 8:35, 37-39
Matthew 14:13-21

Aim

To know that Jesus fed a big crowd of people.

Starter

What's in my lunch box today? Have a lunch box, and a number of lunch items laid out on the floor. The children cover their eyes as you secretly choose a few things to put in the box. Then you ask, 'What's in my lunch box today?' Everyone tries to guess or work it out from the items that are now missing from the floor. When everyone has said what they think, reveal the true contents and take them out, ready to start again.

Teaching

Using the same lunch box, place inside it five little rolls and two sardines. (Be brave and go for real ones!) Set out a green bath towel on the floor, with a cut-out shiny blue lake laid on top of it. Tell the children how crowds and crowds of people wanted to be with Jesus all the time, because they could tell that he loved them. It's always nice to be with people who you know are very fond of you. The way they look at you and the way they talk to you makes you feel happy and safe. That's how Jesus makes people feel.

Well, they had heard that Jesus was going over the lake on a boat. (Make a toy boat go over the lake.) The people didn't have a boat, and they were on this side of the lake. So how could they reach Jesus? Yes, they could walk around the lake! So they did. It was quite a long walk but they were so keen to find Jesus that they didn't mind. Move the lunch box round the lake and put it down on the other side.

When Jesus saw them he was tired. He had actually come for a rest. So what do you think he said? 'Go away, I'm tired'? That doesn't sound like Jesus, does it, and he didn't say it. He made the

people welcome, and healed the ones who were ill, and forgave the ones who wanted to put right bad things they had done, and he talked to them all in the sunshine.

By the evening they were still there, and they were all hungry. So what do you think Jesus did? He fed them. What with? Yes, one person said Jesus could use their lunch. What was the lunch? Open the box to see.

Jesus took what was offered (take it), thanked God for it (thank God), broke it all up (break it all up), and broke it all up . . . and broke it all up . . . and there was loads of food for everyone there, crowds and crowds and crowds of them! And they all shared it. (Share the food.)

Praying

Loving Father,
give us this day our daily bread. Amen.

Activities

The children can sing the action song about the feeding of the five thousand – *5 0 0 0 + hungry folk.*
Here are the actions:

5 0 0 0 + hungry folk,
(five fingers on one hand, make ring with other hand which is shown three times, then rub tummies)
came 4 2 listen 2 Jesus. *(cup hand to ear)*
The 6 x 2 said O O O,
(use fingers for each number and for the O)
where can we get some food from?
(shrug shoulders and open hands, moving head from side to side)
Just 1 had 1 2 3 4 5, *(use fingers)*
loaves and 1 2 fishes. *(count with fingers)*
When Jesus blessed the 5 + 2
(hands face down as if blessing; count with fingers)
they were increased many x over.
(roly-poly with hands going upwards)
5 0 0 0 + 8 it up, *(use fingers, then pretend to eat)*
with 1 2 3 4 5 6 7 8 9 10 11 12 basketfuls left over.
(count on fingers and stamp each foot for 11 and 12)

(From a song by Ian Smale
© Copyright 1985 Kingsway's Thankyou Music.)

On the sheet they can hunt for the hidden loaves and fish in the picture, and model the loaves and fish from plasticine or playdough to wrap in a small square of cloth (cut from an old sheet or shirt). Here is a recipe for playdough. Mix two teaspoons of cream of tartar, one cup of plain flour, half a cup of salt, one tablespoon of oil and one cup of water to form a smooth paste. Cook slowly in a saucepan until the dough comes away from the sides of the pan and forms a ball. When the dough is cool enough, take it out of the pan, add food colouring and knead for three or four minutes. (Store in an airtight container in the fridge.)

LOAVES AND FISHES

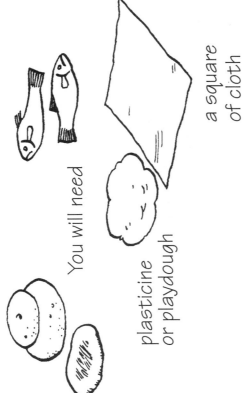

You will need

plasticine or playdough

a square of cloth

Make bread and fish out of the playdough

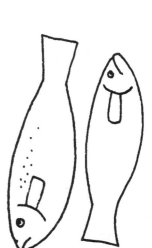

Put them in the cloth

Can you find the loaves and fishes?

For parents to pray with your child

Loving Father, give us this day our daily bread. Amen.

Nineteenth Sunday of the Year

Thought for the day

God is faithful to us through all the storms of life, yet our faith in God is so very small.

Readings

1 Kings 19:9, 11-13
Psalm 84:9-14
Romans 9:1-5
Matthew 14:22-33

Aim

To know that God can cope with our bad days as well as the good ones.

Starter

What's the time, Mr Wolf? The children creep up on Mr Wolf, who sometimes pleasantly tells them the time, and sometimes decides it's time to eat them.

Teaching

Use a few instruments – such as simple shakers and bells, saucepans and wooden spoons, and hand tapping and clapping – as you talk about the different moods of the weather. Sometimes it seems wild and cross, with the wind racing round and blowing everything over, and the rain lashing down. (Make the sounds.) Sometimes it seems in a quiet and gentle mood, perhaps when it's a bit hazy and misty, and there isn't any wind, or when the snow is quietly falling. (Make those sounds.) And sometimes the weather seems all happy and smiley, with the sun shining in a clear blue sky and just a little breeze, and everywhere warm and bright. (Make these sounds.) Sometimes it seems sad, with dark grey clouds and steady rain. (Make these sounds.)

It's the same with us. We have times when we feel all wild and cross, and we grumble and snap at everyone and make ourselves as horrid as possible. Sometimes we have quieter times, when we just want to sit and cuddle up to someone who loves us, and read a story, or watch television, or go to sleep. And sometimes we feel all sunny bright and happy, bouncing around with lots of energy and being friendly and helpful.

Which of those times do you think God loves you best? Answer with a simple 'No' to every suggestion until someone says that God loves us all the time, and celebrate that truth together. Sometimes what we do makes God sad, but he is loving us all the time, in all our different moods.

Praying

Sometimes the weather is wild and cross.
  (shake fists and stamp feet)
Sometimes the weather is quiet.
  (lie down still)
Sometimes the weather is sunshine happy.
  (trace big sunshine smile)
Sometimes the weather is sad.
  (make fingers into trickling rain)
Sometimes I feel wild and cross.
  (shake fists and stamp feet)
Sometimes I feel quiet.
  (lie down still)
Sometimes I feel sunshine happy.
  (trace big sunshine smile)
Sometimes I feel sad.
  (fingers make trickling tears down cheeks)
And ALL the time God loves me!
  (stretch arms out in wide circle all around)
God loves me ALL the time!
  (reverse the wide circle)

Activities

The sheet can be made into a weather chart for the children to set each day. They will each need a split pin, and you may like to make the pointers in advance, from different coloured paper. The chart can be strengthened by sticking it on to thin card.

Notes

1. Colour in the weather pictures
2. Paste onto thin card
3. Cut out weather chart and pointer
4. Attach pointer to weather chart with a split pin
5. Move the pointer to today's weather

For parents to pray with your child

Sometimes the weather is wild and cross
(shake fists and stamp feet)
Sometimes the weather is quiet (lie down still)
Sometimes the weather is sunshine happy
(trace big sunshine smile)
Sometimes the weather is sad (make fingers
into trickling rain)
Sometimes I feel wild and cross (shake fists
and stamp feet)
Sometimes I feel quiet (lie down still)
Sometimes I feel sunshine happy (trace big
sunshine smile)
Sometimes I feel sad (fingers make trickling
tears down cheeks)
And ALL the time God loves me!
(Stretch arms out in wide circle all around)
God loves me ALL the time!
(Reverse the wide circle)

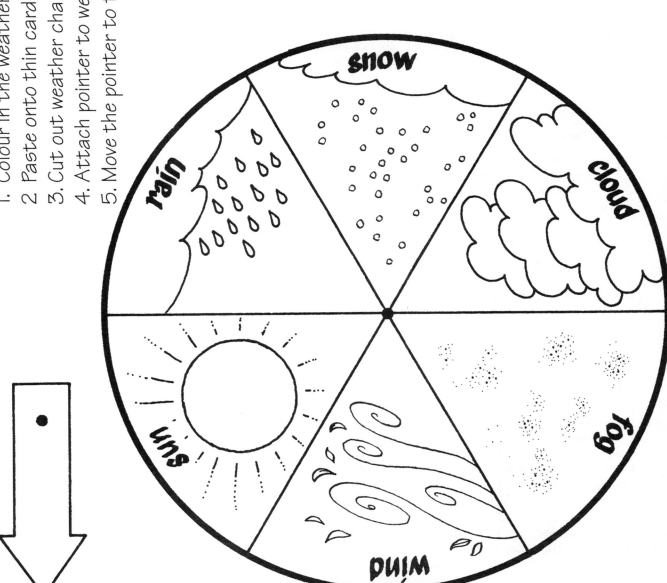

Twentieth Sunday of the Year

Thought for the day

The good news of salvation is not limited to a particular group or nation but available for the whole world.

Readings

Isaiah 56:1, 6-7
Psalm 66:2-3, 5-6, 8
Romans 11:13-15, 29-32
Matthew 15:21-28

Aim

To know that God loves everyone in the whole world.

Starter

The world is turning. Make a circle and choose some children to be birds, some planes and some clouds. Walk round singing to the tune of *The wheels on the bus*:

The world is turning round and round,
round and round,
round and round.
The world is turning round and round
all year long.

As you sing it and walk around again, all the birds can fly around the moving earth. Then the planes can zoom around. Then the clouds can drift lightly around.

Teaching

Bring along either a large globe beach ball, or a globe, and spin it around, pointing out where on our planet earth we are. (Although this age group is too young to understand maps, they can begin to get an idea of living on a round world.)

Talk about the different places on our world where people live. Some children live where it is very hot all the time, and some where it is very cold all the time. Some children live where it rains and rains every day, and some where it hardly ever rains. Some children have never seen snow, and some live in snow all the year round. (Calendars are often a good source of pictures, or you can show them pictures from library books, or photographs you have taken.)

Some of the world is very flat, and some has high hills and mountains. Some children go to church by boat, and some by donkey. Lots of children all over the world walk to church and lots drive or cycle.

And all that goes on at the same time on our round, spinning world! (Spin the globe again.) You know that God loves each of you? Well, he also loves each and every person living in the world. No one is left out.

You can sing the prayer today.

Praying

He's got the whole world in his hand,
he's got the whole wide world in his hand,
he's got the whole world in his hand,
he's got the whole world in his hand!

Activities

The children can make their sheet into a turning world. Beforehand use the land mass shapes as templates and cut these from green and white paper. Also cut out blue circles to fit the basic shape shown. The children can then stick these on. Punch a hole in the place shown so the children can thread a pipe-cleaner through it, and twist the ends together. They can then make the world turn by pushing it along a surface, holding the pipe-cleaner.

Notes

This is what people in space would see if they were looking at earth from the top

1. Colour the world in, using pens, pencils or coloured paper

2. Stick it on cardboard

3. Get a grown-up to make a hole in the middle

4. Thread a pipe cleaner through the middle and twist the ends together

5. By holding the top and pushing it along a surface you can make the world turn

For parents to pray with your child

He's got the whole world in his hand,
he's got the whole wide world in his hand,
he's got the whole world in his hand,
he's got the whole world in his hand.

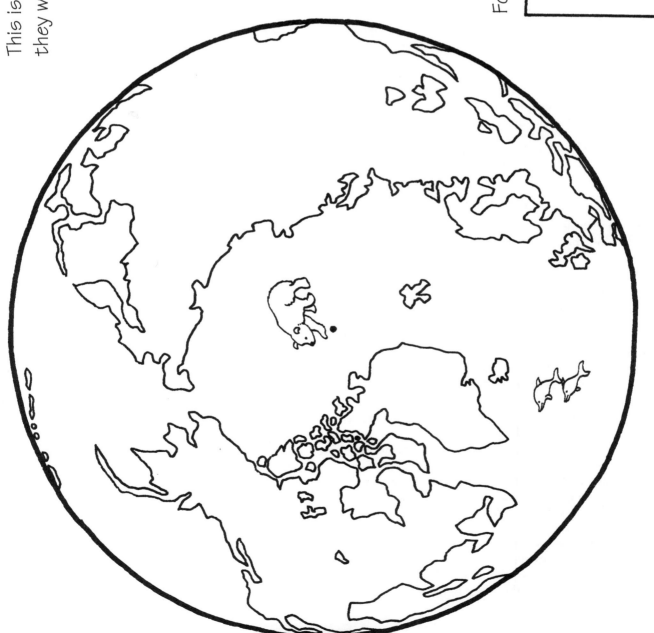

TWENTY-FIRST SUNDAY OF THE YEAR

Thought for the day

The Church is the Body of Christ, built on strong rock of faith and energised by the living Breath of God.

Readings

Isaiah 22:19-23
Psalm 137:1-3, 6, 8
Romans 11:33-36
Matthew 16:13-20

Aim

To know that the Church is made of people.

Starter

Who can it be? Have some large pictures of familiar things, people and places, and start with a picture completely covered up. Gradually uncover it. The children say what they think it is and can see if they're right when it is totally revealed.

Teaching

Have a picture of Jesus healing, or with the children. This could be an illustration in a children's Bible. Start with it fully covered, as in the starter activity, and tell the children that this picture is someone they have never seen, but who they know and love. As you talk, giving verbal clues, uncover the picture so they can see that it is Jesus. They are getting to know Jesus better and better as they hear more about him and as they talk with him in prayer.

Now show a large outline picture of a church. What do we do in church? We pray to God, we sing together to thank God and praise him, we give our money to God, we hear about Jesus, we share a meal, and we play in the children's corner.

What's inside our church? Coloured windows, an altar, candles, flowers, chairs and books.

All those things are there to help us worship God, and to give him our best, as a thank-you for everything God has given us. There are people in church at the moment, and we are all here as well. And there are grown-ups and children all over the world in their churches today. They are all there to worship God and say thank you by giving him their best singing and their best living every day.

Praying

The Body of Christ needs eyes and legs
and feet and hands and mouth.
We are the Body of Christ on earth –
God's eyes and legs
and feet and hands and mouth!

Activities

On the sheet there are puppets to make which the children can work by pushing their fingers through the holes. They can also draw in the missing bits of body.

Notes

98

We are the body of Christ

cut out

cut out

Colour and cut out. Your fingers can be the arms and legs!

For parents to pray with your child

The body of Christ needs eyes and legs and feet and hands and mouth. We are the Body of Christ on earth - God's eyes and legs and feet and hands and mouth!

Help the artist finish the picture

Twenty-second Sunday of the Year

Thought for the day

As Jesus prepares for the necessary suffering of the cross, he is tempted, through well-meaning friendship, to avoid it.

Readings

Jeremiah 20:7-9
Psalm 62:2-6, 8-9
Romans 12:1-2
Matthew 16:21-27

Aim

To know that Jesus is willing to suffer for us because he loves us.

Starter

Have ready some bean bags or rolled socks to throw about, and a basket or bag to put them in. Throughout the throwing activity, ask children by name to do things – 'Ben, will you give everyone a bean bag?' 'Noah, will you throw your bean bag as far as you can?' 'Julian, will you throw your bag as high as you can?' 'Eleanor, will you go round with the basket, and, everyone else, will you put your bag in the basket?' Give lots of praise, thanks and encouragement throughout. Catch them being good as much as possible, tactically ignoring the inappropriate behaviour as much as you can.

Teaching

Explain that the reason they all helped so well during that activity was that they were being kind. If they were selfish they wouldn't have done it. Being kind is doing things for other people, even when it isn't what we like doing best. Sometimes being kind is nice (Will you help me eat up these last biscuits so I can wash the tin?), and sometimes being kind is not so much fun (Can you help me by putting your toys away now?). Collect ideas about times they have been kind and celebrate these.

Tell the children that whenever they are kind they are being just like Jesus. He loves us so much that he was ready to give up everything for us, and put up with lots of hurts. Jesus was kind when he made people better, and when he made them feel safe and happy. He was kind because he helped people and set them free from worrying all the time. He was kind when they were sorry for what they had done wrong, and Jesus forgave them.

It is good to practise being kind, whether we are boys or girls, men or women, and when we do, it makes Jesus very happy.

Praying

Thank you, God, for those I love
and all they do for me.
Help me to be kind as well –
I really want to be!

Activities

On the sheet there are situations for them to look at and think how they could be kind here. They are also encouraged to celebrate the ways other people are kind to them. Also, the children can do something kind today, making some chocolate cornflake cakes to give away.

Notes

In the shops or car

With my friends

With my family

For parents to pray with your child

Thank you, God,
for those I love
and all they do for me.
Help me to be kind as well –
I really WANT to be!

How can I be kind?

Thank you!

Twenty-third Sunday of the Year

Thought for the day

It is our responsibility to encourage and uphold one another in living by the standard of real love.

Readings

Ezekiel 33:7-9
Psalm 94:1-2, 6-9
Romans 13:8-10
Matthew 18:15-20

Aim

To know that God forgives us.

Starter

Provide enough potatoes and spoons for everyone, so that they can try getting from one end of the room to the other and back as quickly as possible, trying not to drop the potato. If the children are at the older end of the age-range you could make this into a race, but that isn't necessary, as it is the exercise in balance and sorting out mishaps which is important. Support those who are hesitant or timid, so they get used to picking the potato up and trying again when things go wrong.

Teaching

Talk about the potato and spoon runs, and how hard it was to manage without getting it wrong and dropping the potato. What did they do to put things right when their potato dropped? They didn't stand and do nothing and they didn't give up. They went after the runaway potato, picked it up and put it back in the spoon. Then they could carry on.

In our life we sometimes make mistakes. Sometimes we choose to do what we know is wrong. Both children and grown-ups sometimes choose to do what they know is wrong. We might have been told to stop drawing on the wall, but we choose to do it anyway. We might see our baby sister is asleep, and we choose to wake her up and make her cry. Lots of the time we choose to do the right thing, but what can we do to put things right when we have done what is wrong?

We can say sorry. Saying sorry means that we wish we hadn't been unkind or disobedient, and we want to put things right. We can say sorry to grown-ups, to our big brothers and sisters or our little brothers and sisters. We can say sorry to our friends. And we can say sorry to God. When we have said sorry, and meant it, God will help us to put things right, and then we can carry on happily with our life again.

Praying

Jesus, when people say to me, 'No!'
and I think, 'I'm still going to do it,
whatever they say',
I know that isn't good, and I'm sorry, Jesus.
Thank you for helping me put it right again.

Activities

On the sheet there are all kinds of things and people in the wrong places, and the children can try sorting out where they ought to be. They can also make a puzzle which can be put together wrongly, but they put it right.

Notes

What's wrong here?

Colour and cut along the lines

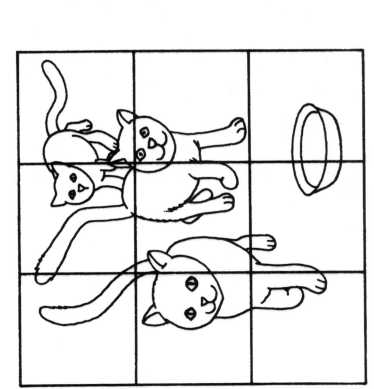

For parents to pray with your child

Jesus, when people say to me,
'No!'
and I think 'I'm still going to
do it, whatever they say',
I know that isn't good, and I'm
sorry, Jesus.
Thank you for helping me put
it right again.

TWENTY-FOURTH SUNDAY OF THE YEAR

Thought for the day

Forgiving is a natural result of loving, so it is not an option for us but a command.

Readings

Ecclesiasticus 27:30-28:7
Psalm 102:1-4, 9-12
Romans 14:7-9
Matthew 18:21-35

Aim

To know that we are to love as God loves us.

Starter

Sit in a circle. One person does something and the next person does the same, then the next until everyone has done it. This might be standing up, turning round and sitting down again, clapping a rhythm or blinking twice. Everyone changes places, and then you start the round again with a different person and a different action.

Teaching

Tell the children that you are going to give them all a present, and that you want them to share the present they are given with everyone else. Make sure they are all clear about this expectation and then give every child a little pack of chocolate buttons, smarties, jelly babies or raisins. It's nice to have a variety, and only have a few sweets in each pack. Now play some music while the children can go round offering other children sweets from their packs. Encourage them to say 'thank you' for what they are given.

Sit in the circle again and talk about the fun of having things given to us, and the fun of giving to others which they have just enjoyed. God gives us his love all the time in so many ways, and we are to do the same – we are to be loving and giving.

Praying

Thank you, Father God,
for the love you give to me.
Teach me how to be like you,
happy to love and give.

Activities

There is space on the sheet for some printing, which passes on a picture all over the place from the master design, and so reinforces the generosity of God's giving. The children will need potato wedges cut into designs as shown, and some flat trays of thick paint mixed with a little washing-up liquid. Ensure their clothes are well protected and have washing-up bowls with warm soapy water and towels at the ready for afterwards.

Notes

God loves giving again and again and again and again!

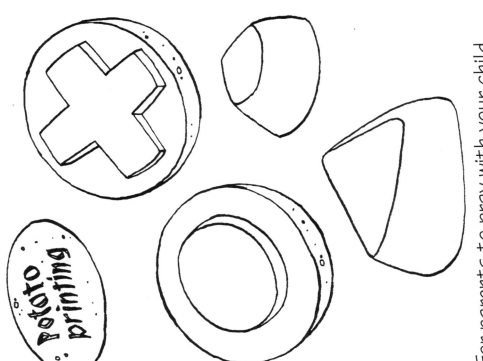

Potato printing

For parents to pray with your child

**Thank you, Father God,
for the love you give to me.
Teach me how to be like you,
happy to love and give.**

TWENTY-FIFTH SUNDAY OF THE YEAR

Thought for the day

We have no right to be envious at the generosity and mercy God shows to others.

Readings

Isaiah 55:6-9
Psalm 144:2-3, 8-9, 17-18
Philippians 1:20-24, 27
Matthew 20:1-16

Aim

To know that God is generous, and when we are generous, we are being like him.

Starter

Play shops, with empty packets and cartons, play money and shopping bags and baskets.

Teaching

When we go out shopping we look out for things that are on special offer. (Show the children some things you have bought this week because there were two toilet rolls for the price of one, or because you got free chocolate bars with your tea bags.) The people who own the shop like to be generous and give things away sometimes so that we shoppers are happy and go back and buy more next time. They end up making more money if they are sometimes generous.

God is generous. He gives away free sunshine and free showers of rain. He gives us free sea and free clouds and free hills and rivers. He gives us life, so we can live in his lovely free earth and enjoy it. God doesn't give us all this because he makes money out of it. God doesn't make money at all. He generously gives us all this just because he loves us. He likes to see us enjoying his gifts, and there's something else he really likes to see.

God loves it when he sees his children being generous like him; when they share and give things away free, and are happy for their friends to have a nice time as well as having a nice time themselves.

When we are generous, we are being like God, and if we get good at giving, we'll end up much more happy than if we tried to keep everything for ourselves.

Praying

Father, you have given us a bright new day
and we would like to spend it in the very best way.
Help us to be generous, giving it away,
helping one another in all we do and say.

Activities

The children can make rubbings of coins so that there is money in the drawn purse on the sheet, and they can make a posy of flowers to give away free.

Notes

For parents to pray with your child

Father, you have given us a bright new day and we would like to spend it in the very best way.
Help us to be generous, giving it away, helping one another in all we do and say.

Our world is full of God's love

Stick green straw on for stalks

My purse is full of money

Twenty-sixth Sunday of the Year

Thought for the day

God longs for us to die to sin and live, but it has to be our choice, too.

Readings

Ezekiel 18:25-28
Psalm 24:4-9
Philippians 2:1-11
Matthew 21:28-32

Aim

To know about making good choices.

Starter

Beforehand cut out blobs from different coloured paper and also a set of small blobs of the same colours. Have the small set laid out on a table at the side of the room and the others scattered all over the floor. Put on a praise tape and let the children all dance around. When the music stops they choose a colour to stand on. One child has been standing with her back to the others, facing the table of colours. She chooses one of the colours and the children standing on that colour blob get a sweet or a sticker. Then another child becomes the selector.

Teaching

Prepare a Y-shaped road junction from paper and lay it on the floor. In one direction have a full pot of honey hidden, and in the other direction an empty pot of honey. Introduce a bear who walks along the road until he comes to the fork junction. He says to himself, in a growly voice, 'Now which way shall I choose? I can go this way or that way. Now let me see.' Invite the children to help the bear choose. They can ask you where the roads go to, if that will help the bear to choose wisely.

When they ask, show them (but not the bear) that one way leads to a full pot of honey and the other way to an empty pot of honey. Now they can talk to the bear, giving him their help and advice. He talks back, wondering if they are really, really sure, and just supposing they are wrong . . . and having other misgivings that a bear might worry about. In the end the bear decides to take the children's advice and finds the full pot of honey, which makes him very happy.

When we have difficult things to choose, God will give us help and good advice. God is good, so what he tells us is always going to help us make a choice that is good.

Praying

Help us, dear God,
to choose the good
and loving way. Amen.

Activities

On the sheet they can make their own road for a bear at home to try, drawing in something nice at one end of the road and something nasty at the other. They can also choose their favourite colours to decorate today's prayer.

Notes

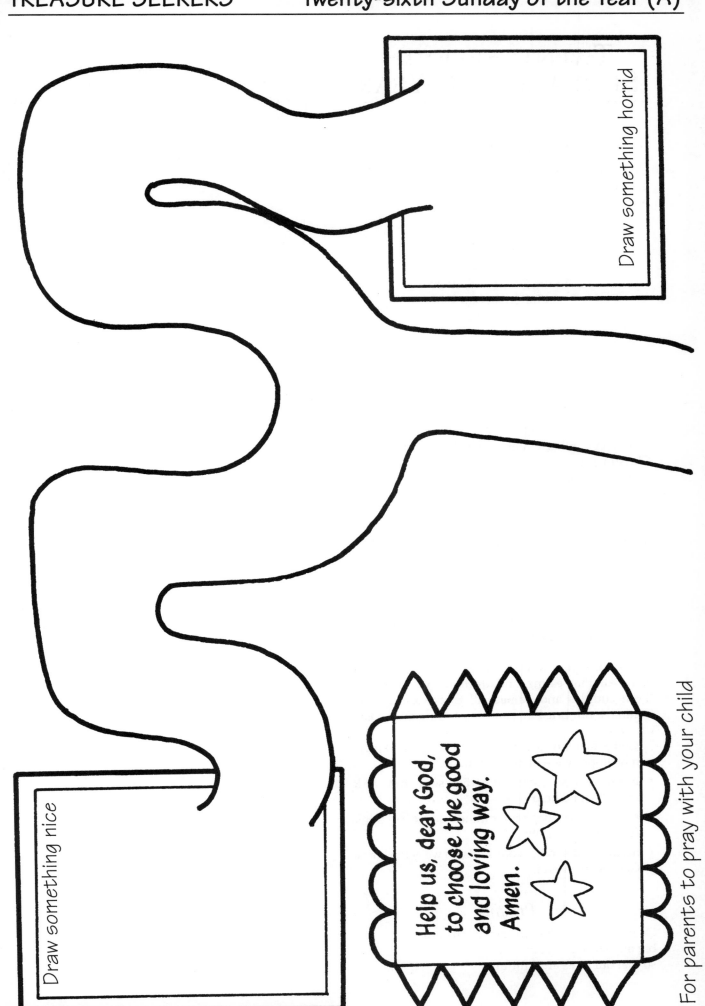

Draw something horrid

Draw something nice

Help us, dear God, to choose the good and loving way. Amen.

For parents to pray with your child

TWENTY-SEVENTH SUNDAY OF THE YEAR

Thought for the day

God does everything possible for our spiritual growth and well-being, but still we can choose hostility and rejection.

Readings

Isaiah 5:1-7
Psalm 79:9, 12-16, 19-20
Philippians 4:6-9
Matthew 21:33-43

Aim

To know that God helps us grow in all kinds of ways.

Starter

Plant some bulbs, either in pots to be flowering at Christmas time or outside to bloom next spring, brightening up a patch of ground near the church.

Teaching

Bring a selection of fruit and vegetables, preferably with a piece of the plant they came from, and let the children look, handle and smell them. You could also eat some. Talk about all the growing that had to go on before the plant gave us this fruit, and the hard work of the farmers or gardeners who looked after the plants so they had enough water, food and light.

We take quite a lot of careful looking after as well. All that eating and drinking we need, all those cuddles and games, all that washing and ironing, tooth-brushing, and comforting after nasty dreams.

God is in all the loving care that we get and give, and he hopes we will grow up to be:

- healthy and strong in our bodies, so we can work and play and help

- healthy and strong in our minds, so we can think sensibly and wisely

- healthy and strong in our souls, so we get to know God as our friend.

Praying

Dear God, thank you for making us grow
big and strong in your love
so that our lives are fruitful.

Activities

The children can make salads or fruit salad with the fruit and vegetables, and use some, such as cabbage and carrot and potato, to print a large picture which has the prayer stuck on to it.

Notes

Stick the prayer here and decorate the edge with prints of cabbage, carrot and potato

Healthy and strong in our body

Healthy and strong in our mind

Healthy and strong in spirit

God
hopes
we will
grow . . .

For parents to pray with your child

Dear God, thank you for making us grow big and strong in your love so that our lives are fruitful.

TWENTY-EIGHTH SUNDAY OF THE YEAR

Thought for the day

We are all invited to God's wedding banquet, but in accepting we must allow the rags of our old life to be exchanged for the freely given robes of holiness and right living.

Readings

Isaiah 25:6-10
Psalm 22
Philippians 4:12-14, 19-20
Matthew 22:1-14

Aim

To know that God invites us to his party.

Starter

Either make party hats as shown below or decorate the room with streamers and balloons.

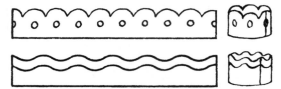

Teaching

Talk about the kind of things they like about parties, and then gather all these things into the happiness of enjoying ourselves together. God's kingdom is like being invited to God's party. He's invited us because he likes us, loves us and wants us to be there with him and all his other friends. Being in God's party is lovely because we are all together with God, enjoying ourselves.

Put on a praise tape, give out some instruments and streamers, and all enjoy worshipping God in a praise party, wearing our party hats.

Praying

Dear Father God,
thank you for inviting me
to your party.
Yes, please, I want to come!

Activities

On the sheet there is a picture of a party to colour, with some hidden things to look for, and a party game to play – putting the tail on the donkey with your eyes closed.

Can you find

For parents to pray with your child

cut out

(eyes closed)

Dear Father God,
thank you for
inviting me to
your party.
Yes, please I want
to come!

Stick the tail on the donkey

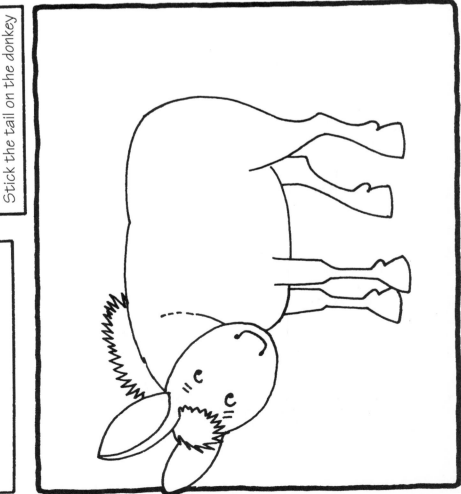

TWENTY-NINTH SUNDAY OF THE YEAR

Thought for the day

All leaders and rulers are subject to the ultimate authority and power of God, the living truth.

Readings

Isaiah 45:1, 4-6
Psalm 95:1, 3-5, 7-10
1 Thessalonians 1:1-5
Matthew 22:15-21

Aim

To celebrate that God's in charge.

Starter

In a circle have a 'news time', passing round a coin, so that whoever holds it is allowed to speak without interruption.

Teaching

Tell the children this story.

'Here she is!' shouted Ali. She was looking out of the window, and could see the baby-sitter walking up to the front door. 'Ding, dong!' went the door bell. Mum opened the door.

'Hello, Vicky,' said Mum. 'They've had their baths, and they know they have to go to bed once this programme ends. Oh, and I've left the mugs for a drink. Sometimes they like hot chocolate, but Jonathan may want a cold drink. Don't let them eat anything after they've brushed their teeth.'

'Vicky, come and see the dead mouse that Molly brought in today,' said Jonathan.

'Sounds great,' said Vicky. 'Hi, everyone! Did your cold get better, Ali?'

'Yep,' nodded Ali. 'But I've got a plaster on my knee. Look!'

'Right, my loves, I have to go now,' said Mum. 'Where did I leave my car keys?'

'You're holding them,' said Jonathan. 'When will you get back?'

'Quarter to eleven,' said Mum. 'Now remember, Vicky's in charge. Look after her and give her a nice evening. Show her where those chocolate gingers are in case she wants some with her coffee. And don't you bring that dead mouse inside again or there'll be trouble! Must go. Love you lots! Bye, everyone, and thanks, Vicky.' Mum hugged and kissed Ali and Jonathan, and Vicky took them upstairs so they could wave from the window.

They watched Mum unlock the car and climb in.

She waved back to them and then Vicky helped them make a drink each. Vicky had coffee with one sugar. Ali had hot chocolate and spilt a bit on the cat, who licked it off. Jonathan had apple juice. And they all had chocolate ginger biscuits.

Talk about people being in charge, and how we can help those who are in charge of us, and how they can help us. God is in charge of the whole universe, and he loves us, and looks after us.

Praying

Lord Jesus,
bless us and keep us safe
now and for ever. Amen.

Activities

On the sheet there is space for the children to draw those who are in charge of them, and instructions for making an orb – the world with a cross on it. Each child will need an orange or apple, two sticks and a wire bag fastener.

Notes

For parents to pray with your child

Lord Jesus,
bless us and keep
us safe now and
for ever.   Amen.

As you draw those in charge
of you, pray for them

These people are in charge of me, to keep me safe

How to make an orb

You will need

two sticks

wire bag fastener

an orange
or apple

1.

2.

GOD'S WORLD

THIRTIETH SUNDAY OF THE YEAR

Thought for the day

We are to love God with our whole being, and love others as much as we love ourselves.

Readings

Exodus 22:20-26
Psalm 17:2-4, 47, 51
1 Thessalonians 1:5-10
Matthew 22:34-40

Aim

To know the summary of the law: Love God, love one another.

Starter

Play 'Here we go round the mulberry bush'. It is a 'looking after yourself' kind of song, so you could have such verses as these: brush our teeth, take a shower, eat a pizza, and wrap up warm.

Teaching

As we sang in the song, we are good at looking after ourselves and caring for our bodies. Our arms are like big machines that we train to pick things up for us and take them over to our mouths. (They can try this with some crisps.) We love ourselves, and that's why we make sure we are comfortable and well fed.

In the Bible we are told two rules:

1. Love God.

2. Love others as much as you love yourself.

When we love others as much as we love ourselves, we look out for *their* needs as well as ours, and want *them* to be happy and comfortable as well as us.

Praying

Dear God,
you have given us life – thank you!
You have given us a lovely world
to live in – thank you!
You have given us people
to look after us – thank you!
You have given us friends – thank you!
You have given us two rules to help us:
'Love God' and 'Love one another'.
Thank you, God!

Activities

Get a drum beat going (a biscuit tin and wooden spoon works well) and clap hands to it. Over this, chant the words: 'Love God; love one another!' until it has become second nature and the children know it off by heart. Then they can colour the two arm or ankle bands drawn on the sheet, and either cut them out themselves or have help with this. Fix them round their wrists or ankles and try the chant again.

Notes

LOVE GOD

LOVE ONE ANOTHER

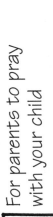

For parents to pray with your child

Colour this picture

Dear God,
You have given us life – thank you!
You have given us a lovely world to live in – thank you!
You have given us people to look after us – thank you!
You have given us friends – thank you!

You have given us two rules to help us:
'LOVE GOD' and 'LOVE ONE ANOTHER'
Thank you, God!

THIRTY-FIRST SUNDAY OF THE YEAR

Thought for the day

Our lives need to reflect our faith; we are not just called to tell the good news but to live it as well.

Readings

Malachi 1:14-2:2, 8-10
Psalm 130
1 Thessalonians 2:7-9, 13
Matthew 23:1-12

Aim

To know that we can preach the Gospel by how we live.

Starter

Sing an action song such as 'In a cottage in a wood' where the actions can take the place of some of the words.

Teaching

Tell the children to look happy, sad, surprised, cross, hungry and tired. Now have them guessing how you are feeling from how you look, giving them a choice of two each time – for example, 'Am I happy or hungry?' or 'Am I cross or am I tired?'

We show each other how we are feeling by how we behave. How do we show that we love someone? We may give them a hug or a kiss, we may look after them and play with them, we may do something nice for them like painting them a picture or helping them. If we said we loved them, but did our best to be horrible to them, that would be silly, wouldn't it?

It's the same with God. We are never too young to tell people about God. We can show people that God is loving and giving by being loving and giving ourselves. We can show people that God is kind by being kind ourselves. We can show people that God is fair by being fair.

Praying

I show I'm happy by smiling.
I show I'm cross by frowning.
I show I love you, Jesus,
by loving those I meet.

Activities

On the sheet they can draw themselves showing God's love by doing something kind, helpful or thoughtful.

Notes

118

For parents to pray with your child

I show I'm happy
by smiling.
I show I'm cross
by frowning.
I show I love you,
Jesus,
by loving those I meet.

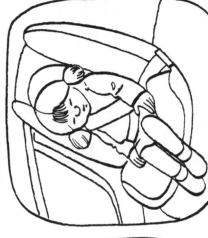

How are these children feeling?

Here I am being kind and helpful.
I am showing God's love.

THIRTY-SECOND SUNDAY OF THE YEAR

Thought for the day

We need to keep ourselves awake and prepared so that the Day of the Lord does not come to us as darkness rather than light.

Readings

Wisdom of Solomon 6:12-16
Psalm 62:2-8
1 Thessalonians 4:13-18
Matthew 25:1-13

Aim

To know that we are called to shine like lights in the darkness.

Starter

Close the curtains, if practical, and give two children torches so that they can help the others to find some hidden milk bottle tops around the room.

Teaching

Point out how useful it is to have some shining lights when we have lost things in the dark. Show the children an oil lamp, fill it with oil and light it. We can shine like lights in the darkness, when we are kind and friendly, thoughtful and generous, when we tell the truth and help each other, when we cheer one another up. That makes the world a happier place for everyone to live in. Like this lamp, we need to be soaked with God's love so that we burn brightly.

Praying

Jesus, keep us shining
like lamps in the darkness,
shining with your love
in the world.

Activities

The sheet can be made into a lantern. Provide shiny red paper for the children to push inside so that it shows through the slits.

Jesus, keep us shining like lamps in the darkness, shining with your love in the world.

For parents to pray with your child

(3) Stick this to other edge

(4) Cut this out to make a handle

(2) Cut here

(1) Fold here

THIRTY-THIRD SUNDAY OF THE YEAR

Thought for the day

The Day of the Lord will hold terror for the wicked and unprepared, but rejoicing for those living in God's light.

Readings

Proverbs 31:10-13, 19-20, 30-31
Psalm 127:1-5
1 Thessalonians 5:1-6
Matthew 25:14-30

Aim

To know that God enjoys giving us gifts and wants us to enjoy them too.

Starter

Pass the parcel. Pack it with a sticker at each layer and make sure that everyone receives a gift.

Teaching

When do we give presents to people? Talk about birthday, Christmas and 'just because' presents that we give to people we love. What makes us happy is seeing they enjoy what we have chosen for them, and enjoy using it.

That's what it's like with God. God loves giving, and he enjoyed giving us the things we are good at. Some people are good at being friendly, or playing football, or cheering people up, or saving their money, or listening, or painting, or learning. Go round the group with the children saying, 'I'm happy that God made me good at . . .' God is happy to see us making the most of the gifts he has given us, and enjoying using them. We can all use these gifts to make the world a better and happier place.

Praying

Thank you, God,
for making us good at things.
Help us to use these gifts
to make people happy.

Activities

There is space on the worksheet for the children to draw themselves doing whatever they are good at, and God smiling to see them enjoying the gift he has given them. They can also fill in the card to give someone else, to encourage them.

Notes

For parents to pray with your child

**Thank you, God, for making us good at things.
Help us to use these gifts to make people happy.**

Here I am doing what God made me good at!

Here is God smiling at me

Dear _____

I'm glad God made you good at

_____

Here you are, doing it!

CHRIST THE KING

Thought for the day

In total humility, at one with the least of his people, Jesus, the Messiah or Christ, reigns as King, with full authority and honour for eternity.

Readings

Ezekiel 34:11-12, 15-17
Psalm 22
1 Corinthians 15:20-26, 28
Matthew 25:31-46

Aim

To know that Jesus is the greatest King of all.

Starter

Pass the crown. When the music stops, whoever is wearing the crown sits still while everyone stands up and bows or curtsies to them.

Teaching

Take along a globe and point out where you all live, and a few other places they might have heard of, such as the USA and Africa. Show the children a picture of our Queen and some other heads of state. These are all very important people. But there is one King who is over everyone who has ever been alive and who will ever live. His kingdom is not a place on a globe. Who can this important King be? It's our friend Jesus! We are friends with the most important King ever.

Praying

Jesus, you are my friend
and you are my King.
You are the King of love.
I want to serve you for ever.

Activities

On the sheet there are instructions for making a flag to wave. Each child will need a stick to fix it on. There is also a picture of Jesus washing his disciples' feet, and the children can spot the hidden crowns.

Cut flag out and glue the edge to a pea-stick

For parents to pray with your child

Jesus, you are my friend and you are my King. You are the King of love. I want to serve you for ever.

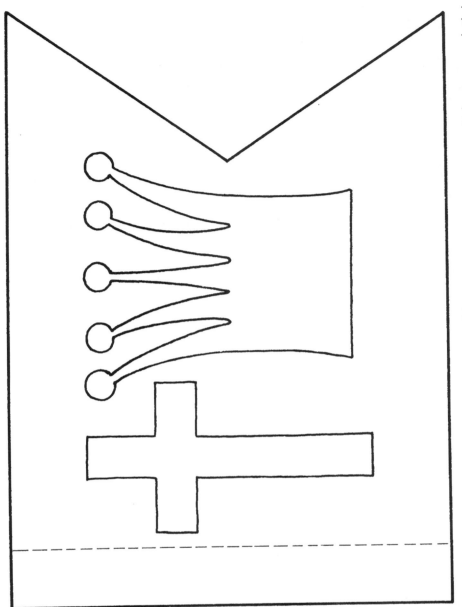

Can you find

?

SPECIAL FEASTS

MARY, MOTHER OF GOD – 1 JANUARY

Thought for the day

Jesus Christ, the Son of God, is born of a woman.

Readings

Numbers 6:22-27
Psalm 66
Galatians 4:4-7
Luke 2:16-21

Aim

To know that Mary is both Jesus' mother and the mother of the Church, the Body of Christ.

Starter

Sit in a circle and pass round a teddy. When each person holds the teddy they say why they love their mum. Then everyone says, 'Thank you, God, for Darren's mum.'

Teaching

Build on the starter activity to celebrate all that our mothers are for us and all they do for us. If you can draw stick people, make quick drawings to represent these ideas on a large sheet of paper, or, having talked about it, give everyone crayons to draw what they love about their mother on a communal sheet, and then share the ideas on it.

What were we celebrating last week? Christmas! Whose birthday was it? Jesus' birthday. Who was Jesus' mother? Mary. It was Mary who carried Jesus inside her until he was ready to be born, and Mary who looked after the baby Jesus, and fed him and kept him clean, and washed his clothes, and cuddled him when he fell over and hurt himself.

We are all part of the Church, the Body of Christ, so Mary is the Church's mother as well as being Jesus' mother. Mary wants us to follow Jesus and get to know him well, and she is always ready to help us get closer to him. Show some pictures of statues where Mary is always showing us her Son. 'Look,' she says, 'this is my Son Jesus. He's the one you need. Do what he says!'

Praying

Thank you, God, for my mother
who loves me and looks after me.
Thank you for Mary, Jesus' mother,
who loves all of us in the Church
and leads us to Jesus.

Activities

There are some pictures of mothers and babies from around the world to colour, and a picture of Mary with Jesus as a small boy, with some parts in dot-to-dot, to be completed by the children.

Notes

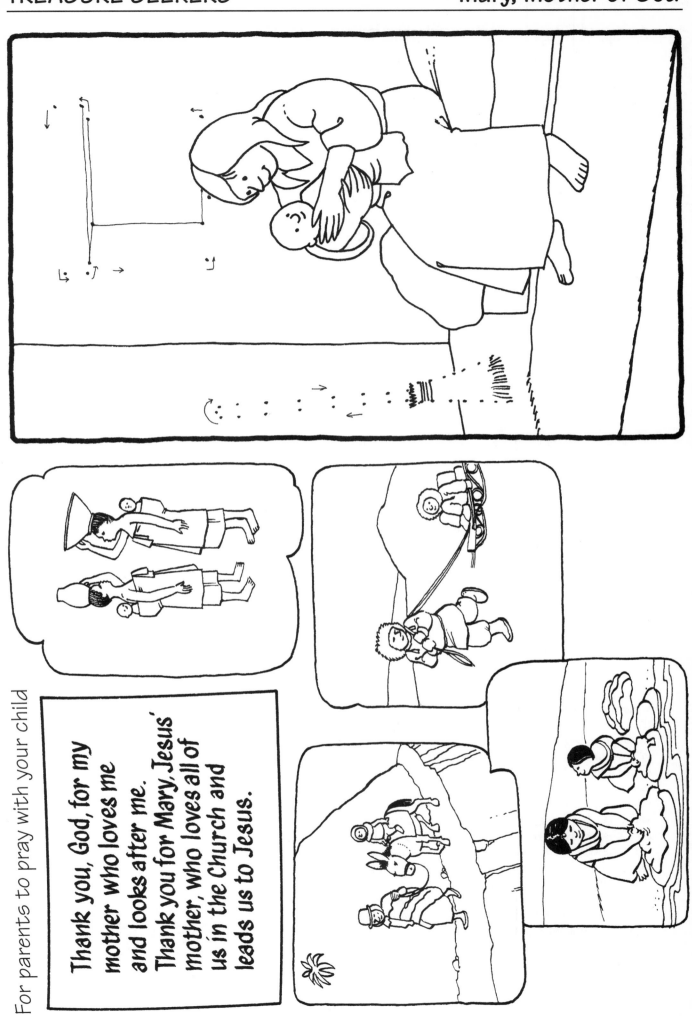

For parents to pray with your child

Thank you, God, for my mother who loves me and looks after me. Thank you for Mary, Jesus' mother, who loves all of us in the Church and leads us to Jesus.

THE PRESENTATION OF THE LORD (CANDLEMAS) – 2 FEBRUARY

Thought for the day

In accordance with Jewish tradition, the Light of the World is presented as a first-born baby in the temple at Jerusalem.

Readings

Malachi 3:1-4
Psalm 23
Hebrews 2:14-18
Luke 2:22-40

Aim

To know that Simeon had been waiting for the Saviour and knew it was Jesus.

Starter

A waiting game. Everyone gets into a space and sits down. The leader calls out, 'Ready . . . steady . . . hop/jump/walk!' and the children mustn't move until they have heard the full instruction. You can make it harder by sometimes giving the instruction quickly and sometimes slowly. Today we are going to meet someone who waited all his life for something, but at last he got it.

Teaching

Dress up one of the leaders as Simeon, or just tell the children we have a visitor today, and put on a headdress and white beard as they watch. When you are ready, resume eye contact with them and say, 'Hallo, children, my name's Simeon. Can you say, "Hallo, Simeon"?' Say you want to tell them about something exciting that happened to you. Tell them how old you are, and explain that you love God and know you can trust him. You knew that one day God was going to send someone to save and rescue people, and God had told you that you would see this Saviour in person before you died. Go on to tell the children what happened on that day in the temple when Joseph and Mary brought Jesus in. Chat your story, involving the children, and try to get across your excitement at actually meeting the Saviour God had promised.

Praying

Leader	Simeon knew he could trust God.
All	We can trust God, too.
Leader	Simeon loved God.
All	We love God, too.
Leader	Simeon knew that Jesus had come to save us.
All	We know Jesus came to save us, too.

Activities

The worksheet goes over the story with a sequencing activity involving cutting and sticking. If you have nativity dressing-up clothes suitable for the children they can 'play' the story through in costume.

Notes

Join the dots to see something that helps you see in the dark.

How is Jesus a light for us?

He helps us see the way to live.

For parents

At home you can help your child stick this prayer on the back of their story, and then pray it together.

Parent   Simeon knew he could trust God

Child/Parent   We can trust God, too

Parent   Simeon loved God

Child/Parent   We love God, too

Parent   Simeon knew that Jesus had come to save us

Child/Parent   We know Jesus came to save us, too

2.

One day God told him to go to the temple.

3.

Mary and Joseph brought Jesus to the temple.

4.

This baby is the Saviour of the World!" said Simeon.

1.

Simeon loved God.

Colour the pictures. Cut them out.

Stick them in the right order on a strip of card.

Tell the story.

SAINT JOHN THE BAPTIST – 24 JUNE

Thought for the day

John is born with a mission to prepare the way for the Messiah by calling people to repentance.

Readings

Isaiah 49:1-6
Psalm 138
Acts 13:22-26
Luke 1:57-66, 80

Aim

To know that today we celebrate the birthday of John the Baptist, Jesus' cousin.

Starter

Messages. Have leaders and helpers standing around the room with notepads and pencils and each with a number of other things visible beside them. These can be anything you like, such as a Treasure Seekers book, a cup and saucer, a bucket, clock, sellotape or tape player – whatever is available. Send the children with messages from one leader to another, like this: 'Kevin, take this clock to Katherine, with my love – here's a note to take with you. It says, "With love from Susan."' or 'Esther, take this note to Kate. She's over there by the window. It says, "Please can I have the Treasure Seekers book? Love from Susan."' Everyone can be trotting backwards and forwards with messages at the same time, and the leaders will be able to see what they can and can't ask for.

Teaching

Thank everyone for all their help in taking those messages – what a busy lot of messengers the Treasure Seekers are today!

God likes using his friends to take his messages to people, and today we are celebrating the birthday of one of God's special messengers. His name is J-O-H-N (sound it out) – John. John's mum and Jesus' mum were cousins, so John and Jesus would have played together when they were little, like some of you play with your cousins. (You might even have some cousins at Living Water.)

God needed John as a special messenger to tell his people an important message. The important message was this: use the same notebook you were using for the starter activity and write on it 'Get ready to meet God's Son!' Read this out to the children. When John grew up to be a man, he waited for God to tell him when to tell the people his important message. At last God said, 'Now!' and off went John, telling his message to great crowds of people: 'Get ready to meet God's Son! Get yourselves ready, everyone!'

Lots of people listened to John, God's messenger, and they started to put right the things in their lives that were bad and selfish. John washed them all in the river as a sign that their lives were made clean again. So when Jesus came, many people were ready to meet him.

Praying

Thank you, Father,
for sending John
to get people ready for Jesus.

Activities

On the sheet there is a large picture of John and Jesus playing together as boys with their mothers. This can either be coloured with paints or crayons or made into a collage using stuck-on coloured paper and fabric.

Notes

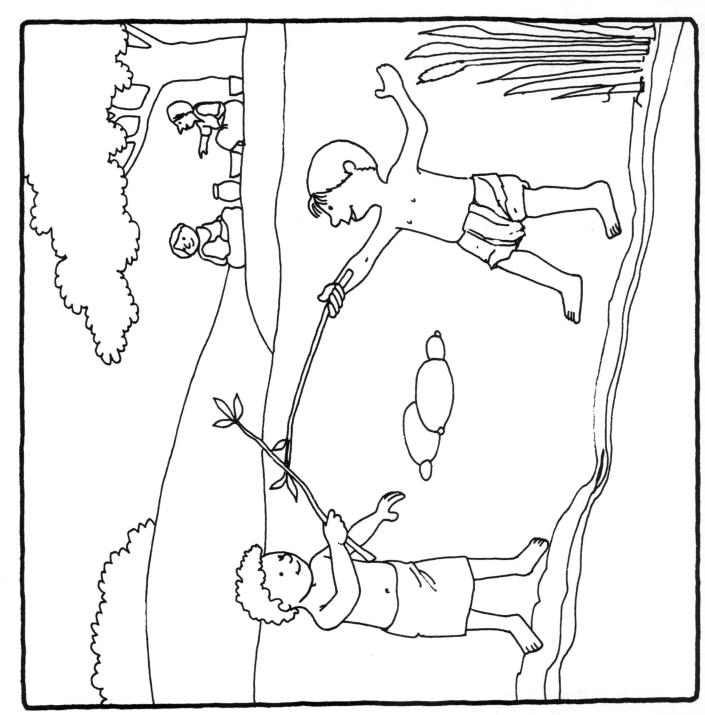

For parents to pray with your child

Thank you, Father, for sending John to get people ready for Jesus.

Colour or stick colours on this picture. Who are the boys? It's Jesus with his cousin, John.

Mary and Elizabeth took Jesus and John to play in the water. They had fun and got very wet.

SAINTS PETER AND PAUL – 29 JUNE

Thought for the day

Through the dedication of the apostles Peter and Paul, the Gospel of Jesus Christ spread and the Church was rapidly established.

Readings

Acts 12:1-11
Psalm 33
2 Timothy 4:6-8, 17-18
Matthew 16:13-19

Aim

To know that Peter and Paul worked together for God.

Starter

Sit in a circle and give the children tasks to do, two by two. Here are some ideas:

- Give one child blue bricks and the other red ones, and ask them to work together to build and red and blue tower.
- Give one child a jug of water and the other a tray of four or five plastic cups. Ask them to work together to fill the cups.
- Give both children a heavy bag with two handles. Ask them to work together to carry the bag across the room.

Teaching

Point out that for all those jobs, both the children were needed. Working together is friendly, and it gets the jobs done better. Talk about those people who all do their own jobs so that together they make a block of flats, run a hospital or a bus. What sort of different jobs are there to do that? (The bus driver, the bus maker, the bus cleaner, the painters, the mechanic and, sometimes, the conductor.) God likes to see his friends working together, like we are now. Talk about the other people who help this to be possible, like the cleaners, builders, helpers, writers, artists and publishers, and our mums and dads.

Today we think of two people who worked together with God to spread the good news about Jesus and lead the Church when it was still very new. Their names are Peter and Paul. Peter was a fisherman and Paul was a tent maker. God wanted both of them to work with him to build the Church of God. And they did. God hopes we will work together in his Church too.

Praying

Thank you, Father,
for working with Peter and Paul
to tell everyone about your love. Amen.

Activities

There are two pictures to colour, one showing Peter and the other Paul. When they have been coloured, they can stick the pictures back to back, punch a hole through and thread wool to hold it by.

Notes

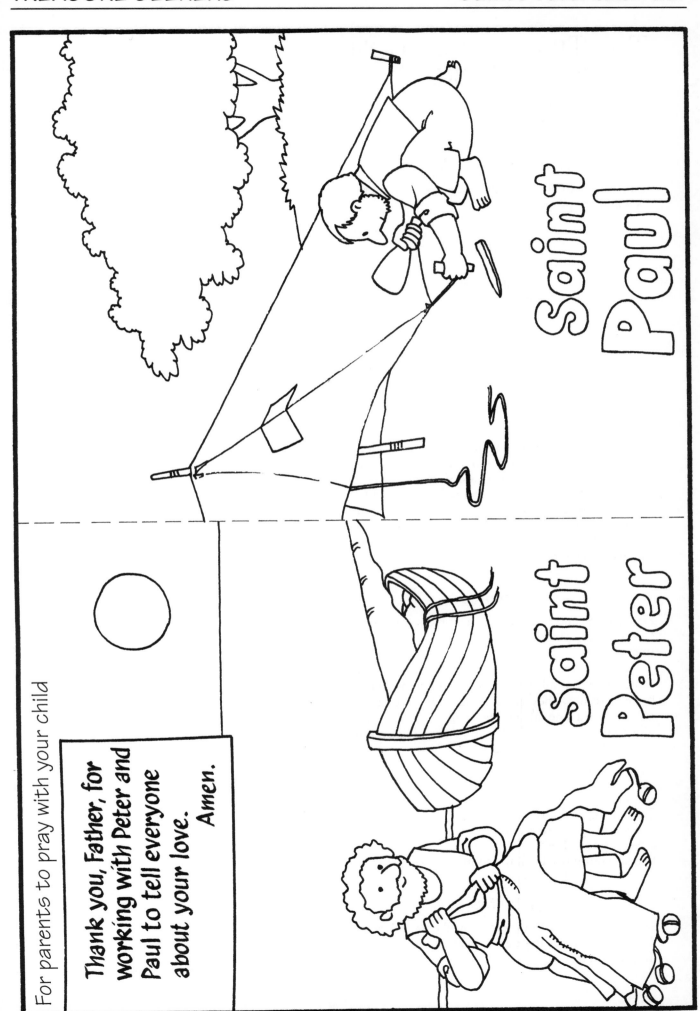

For parents to pray with your child

Thank you, Father, for working with Peter and Paul to tell everyone about your love.
Amen.

Saint Paul

Saint Peter

THE TRANSFIGURATION OF THE LORD – 6 AUGUST

Thought for the day

Jesus is seen in all God's glory, and as fulfilling the Law and the prophets.

Readings

Daniel 7:9-10, 13-14
Psalm 96
2 Peter 1:16-19
Matthew 17:1-9

Aim

To see God's glory in all things.

Starter

If you have access to an outside area, go on a 'glory trail', wandering around looking at things and thanking God for them all. This doesn't just have to be natural things, of course; you can praise God for the people who worked hard to make the path, for those who will be collecting the rubbish from yesterday's wedding party, and for the kindness of the person who mended the broken fence.

Teaching

Sit in a circle and talk about all the places you found God's glory, sometimes hidden and sometimes unexpected.

Give everyone some coloured cellophane to look through so that all the world is a different colour because of how they are looking. Explain that the whole world and all of life is filled with God's glory, but we need to look out for it and listen out for it – otherwise we can miss it.

Praying

Open my eyes, Lord,
to see your glory all around me.
Open my ears, Lord,
to hear your glory in all the sounds.

Activities

The sheet is used to decorate cardboard tubes so that they can focus their gaze on anything and spot the glory in it.

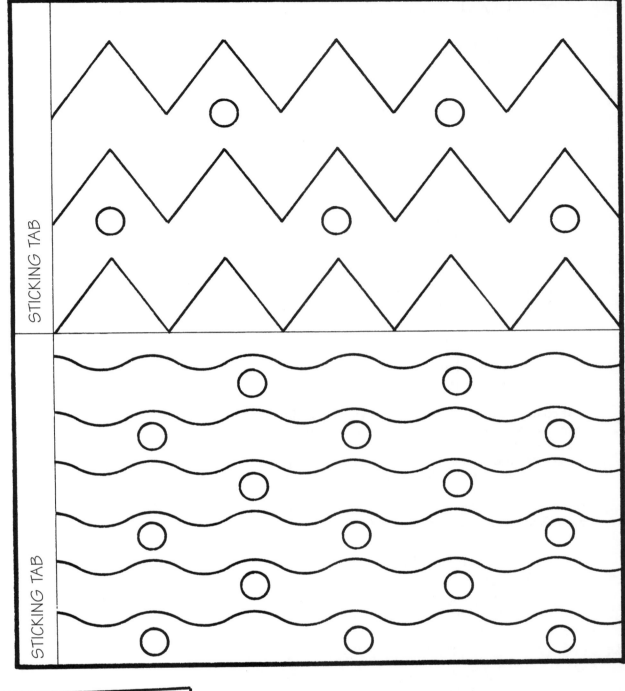

STICKING TAB

STICKING TAB

For parents to pray with your child

Open my eyes, Lord,
to see your glory
all around me.
Open my ears, Lord,
to hear your glory
in all the sounds.

How to
focus and spot
God's glory

THE ASSUMPTION – 15 AUGUST

Thought for the day

The Almighty has done great things for me!

Readings

Apocalypse 11:19; 12:1-6, 10
Psalm 44
1 Corinthians 15:20-26
Luke 1:39-56

Aim

To know that heaven is our home and Mary is there with Jesus, her Son.

Starter

Prepare a number of different home shapes, drawn on slips of paper – for example, a house, bungalow, flat, caravan, house boat, tent, tree house, castle and cottage. Lay them all out and look at each in turn. Say you are thinking of a particular home, and they can point to it when they think they know which one you mean. Start by saying something like: 'I'm thinking of a home which is made of wood . . . has one window . . . and is reached by climbing up a ladder.' Carry on giving clues until most children are pointing to the right home.

Teaching

Homes are where we belong. They are where we go back to when we've been out, and we keep our favourite things there. Talk together about what they like about home.

As well as our ordinary homes that we live in on earth, heaven is our home, where one day we and all our loved ones will live for ever with Jesus. We don't know what it looks like, but we do know that it will be lovely, without any pain or hurts or sadness, and we will be completely happy and at home there.

Jesus' mother, Mary, is there already and will be there to welcome us home.

Praying

Hail, Mary, full of grace,
the Lord is with thee:
blessed art thou among women,
and blessed is the fruit of thy womb, Jesus.
Holy Mary, Mother of God,
pray for us sinners now,
and at the hour of our death. Amen.

Activities

The sheet can be coloured and folded so that Mary is first seen at home on earth and then in the glory of heaven.

Notes

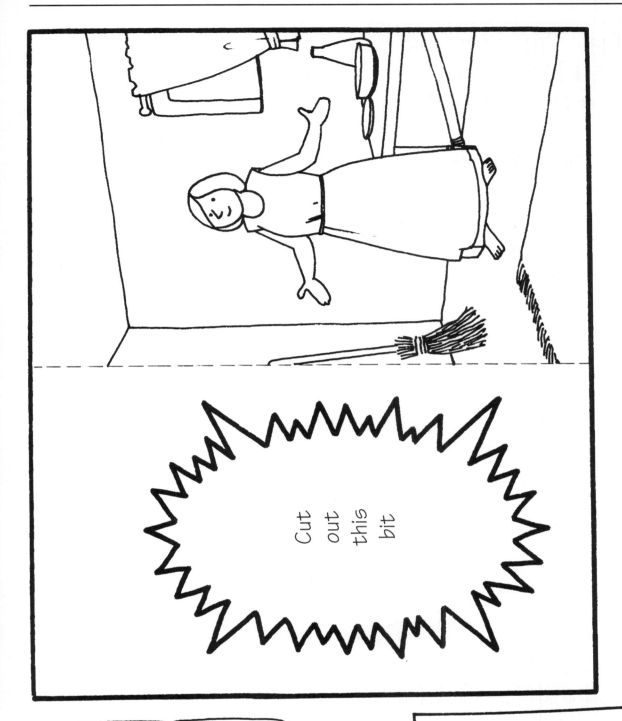

Cut out this bit

Colour the picture.
Have the hole cut out.
On the front of the card
paint bright colours
of heaven.

For parents to pray
with your child

Hail, Mary full of grace,
the Lord is with thee:
blessed art thou among
women, and blessed is
the fruit of thy womb,
Jesus. Holy Mary, Mother
of God, pray for us sinners
now, and at the hour of
our death.   Amen.

THE TRIUMPH OF THE HOLY CROSS – 14 SEPTEMBER

Thought for the day

Through Christ's loving obedience, even to death on a cross, he has opened up the way for us to eternal life.

Readings

Numbers 21:4-9
Psalm 77
Philippians 2:6-11
John 3:13-17

Aim

To know that the cross is a sign of God's love for us.

Starter

Make three signs – one circle coloured in green, one circle coloured in red and one circle with an arrow inside. Have some music to move around to, and while it plays show a series of the signs. They stop for the red circle, go for the green, sit down if the arrow is pointing down and stand up if it is facing up.

Teaching

Talk about signs being useful in our game, as they are on roads. Go over what the red and green lights mean at road crossings, and one or two road signs they have seen.

Have a look at the sign of the cross on various places – such as round a neck, on a building, on a Bible or hymn book. Help everyone to make the sign of the cross on themselves. Why do Christians have this sign? Show the children a crucifix. Jesus is on the cross. He loved us so much that he was even willing to die for us on a cross. Did he stay dead? No! He came to life for ever; he's alive now and will always be alive. The sign of the cross says: God's love is stronger than death. God's love lasts for ever.

Make the sign of the cross again, saying, 'God's love lasts for ever.'

Praying

O God, your love goes on and on and on,
your love will always be.
I sign myself with the sign of your cross,
the sign of your love for me.

Activities

On the sheet there is a bookmark to make in the shape of a cross. Each child will need three strands of coloured wool.

Notes

138

To make a bookmark, colour the cross and cut it out. Punch a hole. Thread wool through hole.

GOD Loves you

For parents to pray with your child

O God, your love goes on and on and on and on, your love will always be. I sign myself with the sign of your cross, the sign of your love for me.

ALL SAINTS – 1 NOVEMBER

Thought for the day

Lives that have shone with God's love on earth are filled with joy as they see their Lord face to face.

Readings

Apocalypse 7:2-4. 9-14
Psalm 23:1-6
1 John 3:1-3
Matthew 5:1-12

Aim

To know that saints are Jesus' friends and followers.

Starter

Sing Oh when the saints go marching in, marching around the room together.

Teaching

Bring along a family or parish photo album and look through the pictures together, recognising some and hearing about others. (This is my grandad who shouted at me when I climbed the cherry tree, and who loved his old dog called Judy. Here's the Brownies at the May Fair, with Mrs Phillips who sells birthday cards after church sometimes. This is Timothy's dad when he'd broken his leg playing football with the youth club.)

All these people are part of the big family of God. We're all God's friends.

Now look with them through another photo album, made up in advance from an enlarged Pebbles worksheet. These saints are all part of the family, too, who have lived good lives as specially good friends of God. Talk about them as you did about the family and parish people, without any 'holy language' reserved for saints.

Praying

Thank you, God,
for all the saints,
your good friends.
Thank you for being
my friend, too.

Activities

The pictures on the sheet can be made into a book of saints, and the cover made from a piece of coloured paper with tissue stuck into it as shown, so that they hold it up to the light and see the light shining through.

Notes

140

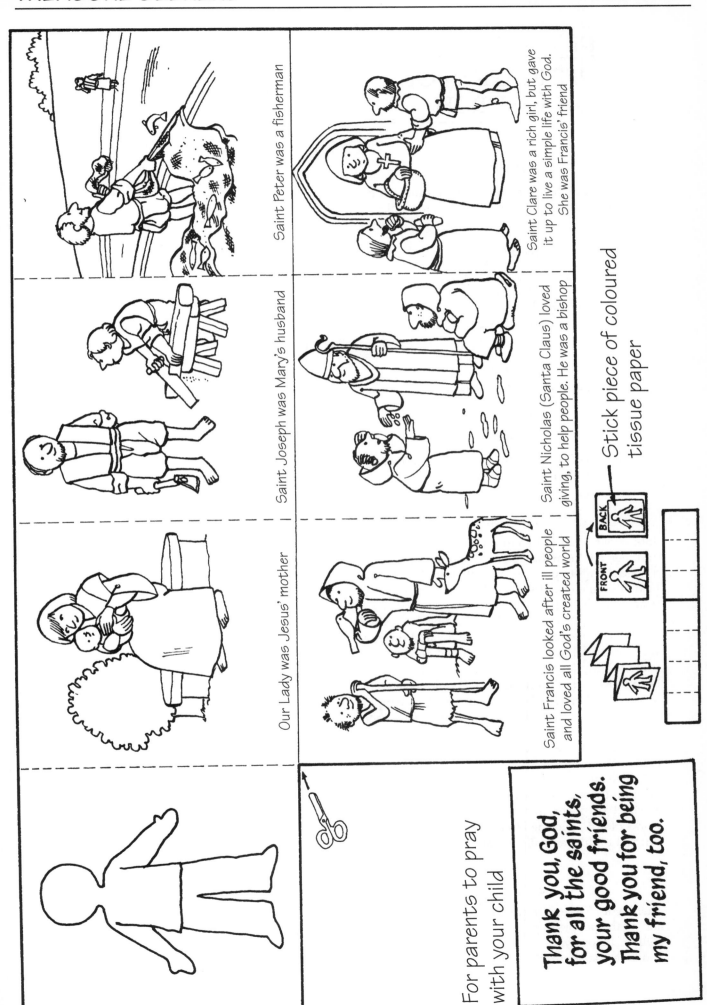

Saint Peter was a fisherman

Saint Clare was a rich girl, but gave it up to live a simple life with God. She was Francis' friend

Saint Joseph was Mary's husband

Saint Nicholas (Santa Claus) loved giving, to help people. He was a bishop

Stick piece of coloured tissue paper

Our Lady was Jesus' mother

Saint Francis looked after ill people and loved all God's created world

FRONT   BACK

For parents to pray with your child

Thank you, God, for all the saints, your good friends. Thank you for being my friend, too.

Feasts of the Dedication of a Church

Thought for the day

The church building symbolises the spiritual temple, being built of the living stones of God's people.

Readings

2 Chronicles 5:6-11, 13-6:2 or Acts 7:44-50
Psalm 83
1 Corinthians 3:9-13, 16-17
John 4:19-24

Aim

To celebrate the building of the church.

Starter

Provide lots of building bricks and/or cartons and boxes, and have a free time of building.

Teaching

Talk about what the children have been building, and then tell them that today we are thinking about a special building where we all come to worship God. It's our church (St. Helen's), and it's now (sixty) years old!

All through the years babies have been baptised here (everyone mimes holding a baby and pouring water over the head), lots and lots of people have come to pray (everyone puts hands together), and been to Mass (hold out hands). People have come here to weddings and been very happy (look happy), and they have come here to requiems when their loved ones have died, and felt very sad (look sad). At our church we've learnt about God and grown to love him.

Which bit of the church do they like best? As they mention things, try drawing them on a blackboard or sheet of paper (they don't have to be expert works of art!), and then thank God together for the church building and all the things that go on there.

Praying

Thank you, Father, for our church
and all the people in it.
Help us to love you
and love one another.

Activities

The sheet can be coloured and folded to make a stand-up church, and if you have pre-cut some people, these can be stuck on to it.

Notes

For parents to pray with your child

Thank you, Father, for our church and all the people in it. Help us to love you and love one another.

You can drink it

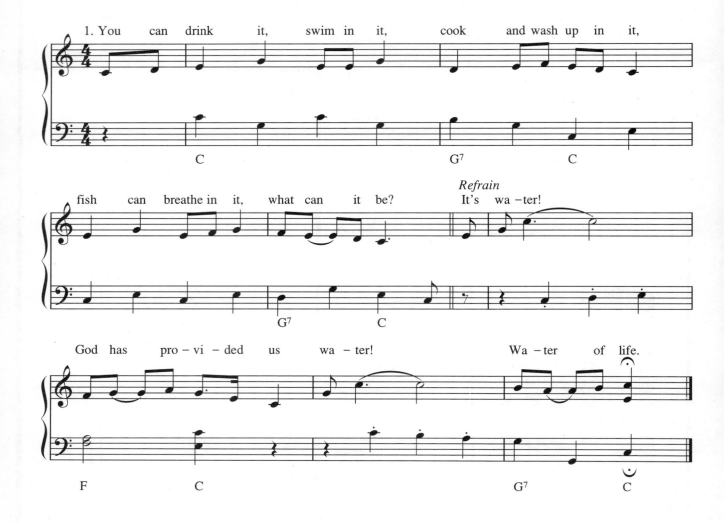

2. It's as hard as rock,
   yet it flows down a mountain,
   and clouds drop drips of it –
   what can it be?

3. It's as light as snowflakes
   and heavy as hailstones,
   as small as dewdrops
   and big as the sea.

Text: Susan Sayers
Music: Susan Sayers, arr. Noel Rawsthorne